Leonard Lee Rue III's Deer Hunting Tips and Techniques

Leonard Lee Rue III's Deer Hunting Tips and Techniques

Leonard Lee Rue III

STACKPOLE
BOOKS

Published by
STACKPOLE BOOKS
5067 Ritter Rd.
Mechanicsburg, PA 17055
www.stackpolebooks.com

Printed in China

10 9 8 7 6 5 4 3 2 1

First edition

Cover design by Caroline Stover
Cover photo by Leonard Lee Rue III
All photographs © Leonard Lee Rue III and Uschi Rue

Library of Congress Cataloging-in-Publication Data

Rue, Leonard Lee.
  Leonard Lee Rue III's deer hunting tips and techniques /
Leonard Lee Rue III.
    p. cm.
  ISBN-13: 978-0-8117-3429-5
  ISBN-10: 0-8117-3429-3
  1. White-tailed deer hunting. I. Title.

SK301.R853 2007
799.2'7652—dc22

2007001001

CONTENTS

ACKNOWLEDGMENTS

In the twenty-four years I have been writing my question and answer column "Rues Views" for *Deer and Deer Hunting* magazine, readers have always submitted far more questions than there was room enough to answer in the magazine. My readers' quest for knowledge is insatiable, echoing my own. The only real advantage to growing older is having additional years of experience, yet I am constantly discovering how much more there is to learn about everything.

I want to thank Krause Publications, the publishers of *Deer and Deer Hunting*, and Dan Schmidt, my editor at Krause and longtime friend, for allowing me to share this information with you. Neil Soderstrom has been my book editor, agent, and friend for many years and works tirelessly on my behalf. Mark Allison and Ken Krawchuk, my editors at Stackpole Books, also deserve much credit for their fine work in preparing the magazine columns for you.

I am indebted to all of the biologists, mammalogists, and other researchers whose work I've relied on and to whom I turn when I have questions. I want to express my thanks and appreciation for my wife, Uschi, whose constant help and encouragement allow me to do what I do. Without her expertise, all of my words and digital photographs would still be stuck somewhere inside my computer and cameras. Finally, I want to dedicate this book to Him who has allowed me to witness His marvelous works and to share them with you.

CHAPTER 1

Feeding

How Many Acorns Does a Deer Eat Daily?

I have long stated that acorns are a whitetail's favorite food, but I never took the time to figure out how many a deer would eat—until just recently. First, I gathered red oak acorns from several trees. Acorns that had just fallen off the tree had green hulls, while those already on the ground for a while had turned brown. The brown acorns weighed slightly less, proving the brown coloration was the result of drying.

On average, 4 green acorns or 6 brown acorns weighed 1 ounce. Because deer will eat both, I arbitrarily determined that, on average, 5 acorns equal 1 ounce, and 80 acorns equal 1 pound. This, of course, is pure speculation. It's important to note that different oak species produce acorns of different sizes. Research has shown that in spring, summer, and fall, deer eat about 8 pounds of vegetation per day for each 100 pounds of body weight. An average white-tailed buck weighs about 150 pounds, and, therefore, requires 12 pounds of food, or roughly 960 acorns per day. Deer almost never eat just one food, however, no matter how much they might favor it. They instinctively know to eat a varied diet. Still, let's assume a buck would eat 800 acorns a day, while a doe might eat 600 acorns a day.

Research in Pennsylvania showed that during a good acorn year, an oak forest could produce about 520 pounds of acorns per acre, or about 46,800 acorns. That would feed six deer for ten days, but we must consider the competition for those acorns. Deer aren't the only ones that love acorns; the nuts are also preferred by bears, squirrels, chipmunks, raccoons, turkeys, wood ducks, and even white-footed mice. Deer prefer white oak acorns because they contain the least amount of tannic acid. After white oaks, in descending order, deer prefer red, black, pin, and chestnut oak acorns.

What Are a Deer's Water Requirements?

Water is essential to life. That's why I believe you'll never find a deer more than 1¹/₂ to 2 miles from water. The amount of water deer require depends on the time of year, the weather, and the area where they live. Deer have a daily requirement of about 1¹/₂ quarts of water per 100 pounds of body weight in the winter, and 2 to 3 quarts per 100 pounds of body weight in summer. In spring, deer require the least amount of water because most of the new, emerging vegetation is so succulent (as much as 80 percent water content) that moisture needs are met through food consumption.

Water requirements are greatest in summer. By late June, does are nursing fawns, bucks are growing antlers, and vegetation water content is reduced. A deer's need for water does not decline in autumn, even though fawns are weaned and antlers are fully grown. This is the period of peak physical activity. The rutting season, with all of its running, chasing, and fighting, requires more water consumption to replace what is lost from constant activity.

Fall is also the time when bucks are almost constantly drooling. The more dominant the buck, the more he drools. Different bucks drool different amounts. I've videotaped some dominant bucks drooling long strings of saliva constantly. Using an eyedropper to simulate the amount of drooling I've documented, I've concluded that some bucks drool more than 1 pint of saliva per day.

I can't say how long a deer could survive without water. I do know that some humans have been trapped without water for seven to eight days, and I'm sure deer could survive as long. If you were hunting in the desert country of the Southwest, it would probably pay for you to set up at a water hole. Throughout most of the United States, however, water is just too available to deer to make such ambush sites worthwhile.

Do Deer Eat Dead Bark?

Deer often eat the bark of live trees, especially aspen, which is highly nutritious. They don't, however, usually eat dead bark. Deer that seem to be eating dead bark are probably feeding on lichens or fungi because they are highly nutritious—some species have protein levels as high as 30 percent. Although a lot of small, dry lichens do not look appealing, many animals seek them. For example, caribou depend greatly on "reindeer moss," a dry, whitish, spindly lichen that crumbles readily in your hand.

Many animals actively seek fungi, and they seem to know how to avoid poisonous varieties. For example, red squirrels pick deadly amanita mushrooms and hang them in tree branches where sun and rain bleach and leach out the poisons, making them safe to eat. Some lichens and fungi only grow to about 1/2 inch, making them hard to see, especially at a distance. Considering this, it makes sense that the deer you saw appeared to be eating bark.

Why Are Acorns Sometimes Empty?

Drought can cause crop failure in oaks. In 2002, I spent part of August and all of September photographing in Yellowstone National Park. Upon arriving home in New Jersey, one of the first things I did was check our acorn crop. I noticed the first black and red oak acorns that fell in October were just empty hulls. I feared there would be a general crop failure, which would have been a direct result of the early-summer drought. After the first week, however, I was delighted to find bushels of meat-filled acorns hitting the ground. Deer gobbled them almost immediately. Then, on October 16 and 17, New Jersey received a major rainstorm that sent acorns to the ground by the bushel. In fact, so many acorns were on the ground that they lasted well into November.

Acorns are extremely high in carbohydrates, which help deer pack on layers of fat for winter. Therefore, our fantastic acorn crop of 2002 undoubtedly helped many deer survive the brutally cold 2002–2003 winter.

Do Maples Produce Good Deer Food?

Maples can't compare to oaks, because acorns are high in fats and carbohydrates. According to Pennsylvania researchers, mature oaks often produce more than 500 pounds of acorns per acre. Maples play an important role, however, when acorns and other mast crops fail. While scouting near my New Jersey home in fall 2000, I found just two acorns all season. A hillside near my home is covered with maples—however—which dropped hundreds of pounds of leaves. In the absence of acorns, deer ate the maple leaves almost as fast as they dropped. Maple leaves are much less nutritious for deer in fall, because they are high in protein but low in carbohydrates, which deer need for winter survival.

Will Deer Eat Baled Hay?

Timothy is a horse hay and is not suited for whitetails. On the other hand, legume hays like alfalfa, clover, and trefoil are much better for whitetails and other ruminants because these animals have the microflora and microbacteria to break down such plants. I have never known deer to refuse baled legume hays during winter when natural food is scarce. Deer don't eat dried hay, however, when succulent natural food is available.

Considering supplemental feeding's disease-transmission risks and the destructive effects of overpopulated deer herds, feeding deer is usually detrimental. Deer should not be fed if their habitat is depleted. Rather, their numbers should be reduced so the habitat can recover. If extreme weather makes feeding necessary, however, you can feed deer any of the legumes I've mentioned. Deer might also benefit from shelled corn, as its carbohydrates will produce more body heat than the protein in legumes. Plus, shelled corn is relatively cheap, providing more food benefit per dollar than any whitetail food I know.

Should I Plant Honeysuckle to Attract Deer?

It doesn't pay to plant shrubs for deer. If it's something they like to eat, they will quickly overbrowse it and kill it. I once planted hundreds of Tartarian honeysuckle bushes for birds. Deer have killed all but a dozen or so. Fence shrubs to let them grow higher than deer can reach, or they will be wiped out.

Tartarian honeysuckle produces such loads of berries that the weight bends the branches down, and then deer decimate them. This is true with all types of shrubs or trees deer favor. Rather than plant shrubs, you'll get more food value for deer by planting birdsfoot trefoil. Check with your county agent to see which variety does best in your area. This trefoil is high in protein, re-seeds itself, and withstands heavy browsing. I can think of no better deer food from March to September. It's a good food year-round, but deer need the carbohydrates of corn or acorns from October through February.

I Saw a Deer Ignore Green Mullein Leaves—Why?

I have noticed a similar phenomenon, and I'm not sure I have the answer. In my home area of northwestern New Jersey, I have seen whitetails eat the dead leaves of white snakeroot and cohosh plants, but they do not eat the green ones. I have looked in several botany reference books and I have found no indication that these plants are toxic in any of their stages. Therefore, I theorize that when the mullein and cohosh leaves are green, there are so many other green plants available that deer don't get around to eating them. Then in late fall and winter, when most vegetation is dead; deer eat the dead leaves because they're all that's available. That might be the case with the deer you've seen.

Any Tips for Good Deer Feed in Georgia?

If you are feeding shelled corn, buy it directly from local farmers. This is much less expensive than buying seed through other outlets. Farmers usually sell shelled corn for about $7 per 100 pounds. Alfalfa is also key, providing deer the protein and roughage they need. Other ideal foods include carrots, apples, and sugar beets, all of which deer love; but shelled corn, alfalfa, clover, and trefoil will provide the most benefit to deer at the least expense to you.

If feeding is necessary, you can start whenever you want. In Georgia, deer probably do not need food until the end of December. In the North, start feeding by mid-November. By that time, most acorns are gone; farm crops are harvested; and natural foods are dead and dry, making them much less nutritious.

Should I Hunt a Cut Bean Field?

I have found deer in my area of New Jersey prefer corn over soybeans during hunting season. Although deer go hog wild over bean sprouts when they emerge, they seldom feed in bean fields when the plants dry. Most combining of soybeans in the Northeast occurs in October and November, and most area farmers harvest corn before beans. Because of beans' late maturation, deer have usually shifted from eating protein, which soybeans are very high in, to eating corn's carbohydrates to build up the fat they need to survive winter. If the farmer has already harvested beans from your field, there is probably nothing there for deer to eat. Therefore, you should hunt near a natural food source.

Can Deer Detect Aflatoxin in Food?

Whitetails cannot detect contaminated corn. Unfortunately, grain with too much aflatoxin for cattle or humans is often sold as wildlife feed. Although the practice is not illegal, it's wise not to feed such grains to deer or other wildlife. You can't see toxins with the naked eye. Grain must be tested in a laboratory to determine its safety.

The Southeastern Cooperative Wildlife Disease Center found liver damage in white-tailed deer that had eaten corn containing 800 ppm of aflatoxin. In Texas, 700 mallards died after eating peanuts with just 110 ppm of aflatoxin. Contaminated grain has also been linked to the deaths of quail, turkeys, and snow geese. Grain from southern states is especially vulnerable to contamination because of extended periods of hot, humid weather. I know of no research that links cancer in humans to venison consumption.

Can Deer Prepare for Winter without Acorns?

Where I live, the poor acorn crop in 1999 occurred because that summer was the driest in decades. Summer 2000 was different, however. The weather was dry in late June and part of July, but late July and August were extremely wet. I thought the excessive rain would produce a good acorn crop, but it didn't. Perhaps the miniature drought in early summer stopped acorn development. Deer will be affected by a lack of acorns. Where I live, however, deer have access to farm crops, hickory nuts, and some beechnuts. But without alternative food sources, deer will be hit hard in winter because they will not have the fat reserves they normally have from eating acorns.

Does Feeding Deer Harm the Herd?

As with most things in life, feeding deer won't cause problems if it's done wisely and in moderation. Keep quantities small enough to avoid concentrating deer in large numbers, and spread it around on the ground so deer don't feed nose to nose. As we've seen in northeastern Michigan, feeding in excess only worsens a herd's long-term health. In Michigan's case, biologists believe widespread feeding dangerously concentrated deer and helped spread bovine tuberculosis.

Other people might worry that you're acclimating deer to people, but that's not the question here. In most cases, you won't physically harm deer if you start feeding them before they're starving. Start your program in November. If a deer has been starving then suddenly has access to corn or alfalfa, it might overeat, bloat, or get rumenitis, a sometimes fatal condition. Researchers dispute whether starving deer have sufficient microflora in their stomachs to process food. I believe, however, starving deer can be given small amounts of food and will be able to process it. The key is using small amounts. I fed starving deer repeatedly using these methods, and have seen no ill results.

If you feed deer, make sure you start by the end of November when their stomachs are working properly and before their metabolism begins to slow. Salt blocks are okay, but I suggest a red mineral block. Deer will not only obtain salt, but also vital minerals.

Ironically, although deer feeding is usually done to help deer herds, the practice can cause more harm than good. For example, supplementally fed deer might abandon traditional migrations vital for winter survival, and instead congregate near artificial food sources. Suddenly ceasing feeding would likely leave deer without a reliable food source, making them vulnerable to starvation. If deer naturally winter in your area, limited feeding might help a few individuals. You must, however, avoid concentrating deer, which increases the spread of diseases such as bovine tuberculosis.

Do Deer Chase Squirrels off Food?

I have seen deer chase squirrels on numerous occasions. Most of the time, it is to chase the squirrels away from acorns where the deer are feeding. I don't recall ever seeing a squirrel chase off a deer. Some might call it play, but I think the deer was protecting its food.

You mentioned the buck you saw chase a squirrel was a fawn. I've noticed young deer chase more frequently because they play more, whereas older deer are more tolerant of squirrels. I have also seen turkeys and deer chase each other off corn.

Does a Great Acorn Crop Mean Huge Racks?

Even under drought conditions, fall 1998 produced a large crop of acorns, including those of the white oak. The drought started in August, but we had an exceptionally wet spring with solid rain for the first twelve days of May. This was when acorns were forming on the trees. The fantastic acorn crop did not affect the size of racks. It added nothing to this year's antlers because acorns drop in September, and antlers are finished growing in August. The fantastic acorn crop, however, did allow deer to go into the winter in excellent shape.

In the case of a mild winter, bucks might produce outstanding antlers because they will get through the winter in above normal condition. There were exceptional antlers in 1998 because the winter of 1997–1998 was unusually warm, allowing deer to emerge in excellent shape. Antlers on New Jersey bucks are also getting bigger because bucks are getting older. Although I hate to see the fragmentation of farmlands and woodlands by suburban development, it often works to the deer's advantage. New Jersey law states that deer cannot be hunted within 400 feet of a house, so there are huge blocks of land where hunting is prohibited. If bucks stay in these areas, they grow older and have larger racks. Eventually, some big bucks leave the protected areas during the rut and are shot.

Why Do Deer Ignore My Great Planted Clover Patches?

Deer would move from the area if there wasn't protective cover. You mentioned, however, you also have small thickets of greenbrier and honeysuckle, which also make good deer food. I can't imagine why deer won't at least feed in your clover patches, even if they don't stay. Is the surrounding area so ideal that it supplies everything a deer needs?

Ask yourself these questions: How many others hunt the land? Could it be overhunted? Are dogs running loose on the property? Is the land more than a mile from water? You're doing everything right to make the acreage a haven for deer. There is just some outside influence keeping the deer away. Continue what you're doing while you search for clues to the answer.

Are Whitetails Browsers or Grazers?

Although deer feed more on farm crops and grasses than on browse, I believe deer are basically browsers that are often forced to eat farm crops and grasses in the absence of browse. A deer's favorite food is acorns, but it also favors berries, apples and other fruits, and mushrooms. A deer prefers forbs and broad-leafed plants over grasses, even though it will eat a lot of grasses. Legumes—such as alfalfa, clover, trefoil, and soybeans—are avidly eaten. Corn is also a preference.

A deer is sometimes described as an opportunist, instead of a grazer or browser, because it's known to devour so many foods. In the northwestern United States, deer eat more than 650 different foods. I still believe, however, that given a choice deer prefer to browse on leaves and new twigs.

Many studies on whitetail diet were done fifty to sixty years ago when most states were rebuilding their herds. Today, deer herds have reached or exceeded the carrying capacity of the land, thus straining certain food sources. Today's studies on deer diet are based on availability, not preference.

Can Deer Hear While Chewing?

Chewing interferes with a deer's hearing because the jawbones conduct sound internally to the ears. Deer, and all other prey species,

Deer usually eat twigs no larger than the size of wooden matchsticks when browsing.

are at a distinct disadvantage when they eat because they are distracted and their ability to hear is lessened. So, deer adjust by gathering a lot of food quickly. Most deer feed in the open for about forty minutes at most, and then retire to safety where they can chew their food while watching for danger.

Do Deer Ever Use Foraging Lines?

While turkeys deliberately form a foraging line, deer do not. If deer feel unpressured, they usually enter a field at a trot as if they are eager to feed. The group then spreads out, giving the appearance of a foraging line. In reality, it's more of an expanding circle. Deer don't feed in one spot, but are constantly on the move, which prevents overgrazing. A bite here and there effectively prunes vegetation, which usually strengthens the plant. Also, by constantly moving, deer force predators to keep moving if they plan to attack. Every time a predator moves, a deer has a better chance of noticing it.

Chewing on the overhead vine, this buck is depositing his salivary scent.

Deer often stand at the edge of a field looking it over carefully before stepping out into the open.

Is Salt Healthful for Deer?

Salt is needed in a deer's diet. In fact, in many parts of the world, man and animals are actually starved for it. For humans, too much salt can cause elevated blood pressure. This does not happen with wildlife because when their need for salt has been filled, they simply stop eating it.

I suggest putting out a mineralized salt block because it helps produce deer with large bodies and antlers. I use a mineral mix blended with red granulated salt from my local feed store. At first, I dug a hole for the mixture, but now I just pour the mixture in the holes the deer have made. Be sure to check with your state's hunting regulations before placing salt licks on your property.

I Plant Rape, Rye, Rye Grass, Clover, and Peas on My 55 Acres but Still No Deer—How Come?

You are doing many things right, but there are still several factors to consider. First, a deer's home range is 1 to 2 square miles, meaning 55 acres are only $\frac{1}{20}$ of its territory. Because of this, it's impossible to hold deer exclusively on your land. You can attract deer, however, and your plantings should do that. Your lack of deer sightings is probably caused by a shortage of deer rather than neighbors' plantings, as you wrote you suspect. If your neighbors have been planting crops and feeding deer for years, deer might not use your food plots because they are accustomed to feeding elsewhere. Low deer numbers, however, are more likely the problem.

Regarding crop selection, some plantings work better in certain areas. Cornell University found that birdsfoot trefoil is one of the best crops for deer in New Jersey, where I'm from. Contact your local agricultural extension office to find out which crops will grow best. A farm co-op should have the seed the extension office recommends.

Putting out minerals is an excellent idea, no matter where you hunt, because most soils lack minerals or have been depleted through farming practices. I put out Deer-Lix, which I mix with granulated red mineral salts for excellent results. Although molasses attracts deer, it is usually too much hassle unless mixed into pelletized feed. Agway's Crunchy 16 is an excellent deer food with enough protein to grow big-racked, big-bodied deer.

What Do Browse Lines Indicate?

Deer are browsers, and they prefer to eat good browse over all other types of food. Deer feed mainly on farm crops during certain times of the year because crops grow where browse might have been available years ago. That supports my contention that we have more deer now in the eastern half of the United States than we have ever had. In pre-Columbian days, most of the eastern half of the United States was blanketed with mature forests, and deer were scarce. Whitetail populations increased when these virgin forests were burned extensively by American Indians, the first game managers.

Deer are creatures of edges, not mature forests. It was these browse-lined edges that provided the nutrients deer needed to flourish. When deer feed along a heavily used browse line, they are feeding on foods they prefer to eat—even if it's scarce or hard to reach. Unless a branch dies from having all of its leaves eaten, it will continue to grow each year. Many of the lower branches grow downward, and most of them will be bent by the weight of their new growth. This brings them within reach of deer. Deer eat along such browse lines more heavily after a rain, when the water's weight bends branches even further.

Heavily used browse lines can be seen along other edges as well. For example, where I live, Tartarian honeysuckle bushes are common. In a conservation effort to grow more habitat and food-producing shrubs for birds during the late 1940s, millions of these bushes were planted. Since then, they have provided excellent food and cover for many types of wildlife. Birds have spread the seeds widely. Deer love to browse on the leaves, and, in many areas, honeysuckle bushes are highly trimmed by browse lines.

Do Deer Eat Peaches?

Yes, and they don't have to be hungry. All they need is the opportunity. Whitetails do have favorite foods, however, and apples are one of them. Deer do not eat peaches as readily as they eat apples, nor do they actively seek woody browse when apples are abundant.

Do Deer Eat Grass?

Deer will eat grass, but it's not a preferred food. Deer are primarily browsing animals. They prefer to eat the leaves off brush and trees, as well as everything else. In fall, deer seek acorns over grass and browse because they produce fat reserves. Deer especially turn to grass where populations are high. A large deer herd will soon over-browse an area, which leaves grass as the next best food source.

CHAPTER 2

The Rut

How Should I Use a Grunt Call during the Rut?

You won't get a lot of bucks to come to a call. If you get a response once out of every five times you call, as you write; you're doing extremely well. I used to advise people to roll the O-ring on the call to the end to produce the lowest, raspiest call. I've changed my mind because I'm finding I get a better response with a slightly higher pitch. I believe that using a low, raspy call might scare young bucks away.

I hear bucks grunt most frequently when they track does. They walk with their heads down and their tails up, and they make a short 3- to 5-second grunt about every ten steps. Start by making soft grunts in case there's a buck hidden nearby. Call every 5 seconds for a minute, then stop for at least ten minutes and watch carefully. Realize that by calling, you're helping a buck pinpoint your position. You have to see the buck before he sees you. Keep motion to a minimum. If, after ten minutes, you haven't had any response, blow the grunt tube a little louder. Always wait at least ten minutes between each series of calls. If no bucks come in, you have to change your location. During the rut, bucks move widely.

A grunt that most people don't even know about is what I call the grunt/moan. This is most often done by a buck that is tending a doe that is not ready to stand for him. The grunt/moan is usually done in frustration and is a long, moaning grunt lasting twenty to thirty seconds or more. The pitch often rises in the middle of a long grunt. When the doe moves and the buck has to move to head her off, he will usually make this moaning grunt.

What Scents Should I Use during the Rut?

Although doe-in-heat scents are good during the rut, do not use them before the time when the pre-rut begins heating up. Before that time, use food scents, such as apple and white oak acorn. Aside from luring deer during the rut, scents can help conceal your odor. Fox urine, for example, is a good cover scent. Deer smell it frequently and aren't threatened by it. Plain whitetail urine is another good cover scent and attracts bucks and does of all ages.

Manufacturers have recently introduced some unconventional scents, such as semen and interdigital gland odors. After dabbling with the latter in the past, I've found that they're best used by only the most experienced hunters. For example, when used improperly, interdigital scent can spook whitetails.

Do Lesser Bucks Breed Any of a Herd's Does?

Researchers have proven that small-racked yearling bucks breed a good percentage of does each year, regardless of the herd's sex ratio or age structure. You can, however, rest assured knowing that this is not detrimental to the herd's overall health. Those runty forkhorns and 6 pointers have the exact same genes that they will have when they reach maturity. They just haven't lived long enough to have grown large racks. It's that simple—age is a most important ingredient to antler development.

It must also be remembered that does contribute to 50 percent of the gene pool. Furthermore, mature does prefer to breed with larger bucks because they instinctively know their offspring will have the greatest chance of survival. It should also be noted that the whitetail's estrous season is synchronized in that most does are bred during the three-week period from November 7 to November 28 (for areas north of the Mason-Dixon line). Doe fawns that breed usually do so during the period from December 1 to December 15.

This young buck has good genetics but needs age to produce large trophy antlers.

This yearling buck is attempting to remove the velvet from his antlers by chewing on it.

The so-called "window of opportunity" for adult does is absolutely necessary because the peak of birthing for the northern deer occurs between June 1 and 21. These dates are optimal because vegetative growth has not yet peaked, and new growth is much higher in nutrition than that found in mature plants.

The breeding season is longer in areas south of the 32nd parallel. Consequently, the birthing season is also longer, but neither the temperature nor the vegetation components are as critical as they are in the North. Because southern deer are not as synchronized (i.e., does enter estrus over longer time periods), it would appear that dominant bucks would get to breed more does. Studies have shown, however, this is not true. In the South, I believe it is exhaustion that prevents dominant bucks from breeding more of the does. The round-the-clock tending of an estrous doe is so demanding that

Bucks, after rubbing a sapling, frequently eat the loosened bark and smell the forehead scent they have just deposited.

many dominant bucks become tired and, in turn, create breeding opportunities for younger bucks.

What's the Purpose of a Rub?

There is absolutely no doubt that the first time a buck rubs is to remove velvet from his antlers. Also, I am just as sure that bucks rub their antlers because the drying velvet starts to itch, just as a person starts to scratch sunburned dead skin. Many bucks start to remove velvet from their antlers during the last week in August, but their necks don't start to swell—sure sign of the rut—until the first or second week in October. Most rubs are made to indicate a buck's presence.

Bucks occasionally mount other bucks to show dominance. It is not necessarily a sexual behavior.

Do Bucks and Does Yard Together after the Rut?

Bucks and does do yard together, but bucks tend to stay on the outer periphery, while does and fawns favor the core areas. This separation within a yarding area probably occurs because bucks and does would have gone their separate ways after the rut if winter had not necessitated yarding; and even in the yard, the instinct is to remain separated.

Research has shown that the melting of confining snow triggers deer to leave yards. If another snowstorm should hit as deer are leaving the yard; the deer that have already left the yard, but are still in the area, will return to the yard.

Should I Hunt a Doe's Chosen Breeding Area?

I never said a doe has a chosen breeding area because she doesn't. What a doe has is a home range that she doesn't want to leave because she knows each topographical feature so well. She also knows what foods are available and when. I have always said that if you want to locate the biggest bucks, find out what the does are eating. Does will be where the food is, and bucks will be where the does are.

Deer do not use their entire home range at one time. They move from one section to another in response to food availability, water, and cover. Does feed in the same area year after year at about the same time because the same foods should be available in the same areas at the same time each year. It certainly would be a good place to set up during the rut. This is why some areas remain hot spots year after year.

When Do Does Enter Estrus?

White-tailed does in Pennsylvania, for instance, usually enter estrus between November 7 and November 17, and the rut usually peaks between November 9 and November 17. Does are in estrus for only twenty-four to twenty-eight hours. Does that do not breed, or do not conceive during their first estrous period, will recycle and come into estrus 28 days later.

It's unusual for a doe not to be bred by her second estrous cycle, because northern fawns must be born between May 15 and June 15 to take advantage of warm weather and the lush protein

Even the dominant bucks seldom get a chance to breed more than six does during the rutting season because of the time they invest in courting each estrous doe.

content of the succulent vegetation. Fawns that are born in July do not achieve the body growth needed to survive a hard winter. A late birthing can handicap them throughout their lives, and they might have a lower ranking in the dominance hierarchy.

Does are capable of recycling at least six times and perhaps more. For example, I once had a captive doe that I didn't want bred, so I kept her in a separate pen. My biggest buck dropped his antlers in January. On April 1, I returned the doe to the research herd. Then, on April 8, the buck bred her. The April breeding means the doe definitely entered estrus for six complete cycles. It also means that although the buck's testosterone levels had dropped and his antlers had been cast, he was still able to copulate six months after the peak of the breeding season. That doe gave birth on October 23, which proves the buck still had viable sperm. And, although the average gestation period for whitetails is 203 to 205 days, the doe delivered in just 198 days, because she wasn't stressed by winter weather.

During the Rut, a Buck Stood in My Driveway, Even When I Shined a Flashlight at It—Was It Blind?

There are no absolutes in the world of white-tailed deer, but several factors might explain what happened. First, when you saw the buck, the rut in your area had been in full swing for about three weeks. During the rut, bucks lose much of their usual caution and do things they wouldn't do under normal circumstances. Second, you mentioned you and your wife had seen the buck before, which indicates the buck frequents the area. With this in mind, the buck might have felt safe because he saw you before and didn't view you as a threat. Third, with the rut in full swing, the buck probably wasn't on a normal feeding schedule. The fact he was feeding on lawn plants might indicate he forced himself to eat where he felt safe and comfortable. Finally, the buck was probably tired or at least in less than optimum condition. The fact he had half a rack indicates he was a fighter. It's possible the buck was involved in a "knock-down-drag-out" fight and was recuperating in the woods near your home.

On a side note, a deer's eyes reflect light when incoming light strikes the tapetum at the back of the eye and reflects back through the eye. If the deer did not look directly at the light that's probably why its eyes would not "shine." I doubt the deer was blind, because you mentioned he had no trouble walking. All things considered, I believe you encountered a rut- and hunger-crazed deer that was grabbing a bite to eat in a place he knew was safe.

How Can I Tell If a Doe Is in Heat?

There's no way to tell if a doe is in estrus unless you see her being followed consistently by a buck. During the rut, bucks check every doe they encounter, but they only stay with those that are ready to breed. If a buck stays with a doe, she is either in estrus or about to enter estrus.

Bucks will often be with a doe for twenty-four hours before she comes into estrus; they will stay with her for the twenty-eight or so

Does squat much lower than bucks do when urinating.

hours that she is in estrus and perhaps will stay with her for six to twelve hours after her estrous period. A doe that's bred and does not conceive recycles back into estrus every twenty-eight days. I always take the urine out of the bladder from does I shoot. Biologists have proven, however, that if you take the urine directly from the doe's bladder, even if she is in estrus, it will not have pheromones in it unless it passes through her vagina.

Bucks are not capable of breeding all year long. Ordinarily, bucks start to breed at the end of August, when their testosterone levels rise high enough to cause their velvet to peel from their antlers. A doe is not capable of breeding until she enters estrus.

Testosterone levels of most bucks drop about the end of December in the northern three-quarters of the United States. Bucks usually shed their antlers by the end of February, but some don't shed until March. One of my bucks dropped his antlers in January and bred a doe in April, which is unusual, but the doe gave birth 198 days later. Usually bucks do not have viable sperm from March to August.

Buck urine is a good attractant and cover scent. It does not matter whether the urine is from a buck in the rutting season or not. Bucks respond to another buck's urine because they consider any strange buck urine to be from a potential competitor.

Does Moon Phase Affect the Rut?

Although the moon's influence on the rut has been discussed in thousands of articles and several books during the past decade, I believe such findings are false. In fact, a panel of the nation's top deer biologists recently concluded that moon phase plays no role in the rut's timing. For years, I have maintained the rut's timing is determined by photoperiodism—the amount of daylight. I base this conclusion on the principle that the rut is timed so each region's birthing corresponds with warm weather and abundant food, which lactating does and newborn fawns need for survival.

In Texas, for example, the rut is later than in the North. This coincides with summer rains, which stimulate nutrient-rich vegetation. Photoperiodism affects the timing of almost everything in nature—molting, breeding, migrations, blossoming in plants, and more.

That's not to say the moon doesn't affect deer. For example, I've found that deer move less during daylight when the moon is full. During such periods, deer bed earlier in the morning and feed later in the afternoon. As hunting pressure increases, deer become almost nocturnal and feed mainly at night—moon or no moon. I don't, however, think moon phase affects the rut's timing.

I believe the emphasis on moon phases has been blown out of proportion. I haven't found that the full moon affects the peak of the rut. Instead, I believe the rut is basically determined by photoperiodism, the declining number of daylight hours in a twenty-four-hour period. Many dark, stormy days in October can fool the deer's pineal gland to believe the days are shorter, allowing the peak of the rut to begin one to two days early. For most of the United States north of the 32nd parallel, the peak of the rut is from November 7 to November 12 or 17.

If deer were governed by the moon phase, then all does would peak at the same time. Southern deer not only have a much longer peak breeding period, but it is also later. We say that does are on a lunar cycle because if a doe is not bred, or breeds and does not conceive during her first estrous cycle, she will recycle twenty-eight days later. This term is used because the moon is also on a twenty-eight-day cycle. But the phases of the moon do not determine when the doe recycles, because it is not what triggers her estrous cycle in the first place.

What's the Purpose of Tarsal Gland Urination?

Deer have forehead, preorbital, nasal, salivary, preputial, interdigital, tarsal, and metatarsal scent glands, making them virtual walking scent factories. Not surprisingly, scent is the deer's primary means of communication. Scent signposting is a form of advertising for deer—like humans putting up billboards along the highway. And unlike visual and vocal communication, scents work for hours to several weeks.

Usually, the sender and the receiver of these olfactory messages don't see each other—and might never see each other. The message, however, is received. Deer deposit forehead, nasal, salivary, and preorbital scent on branches and rubs, and they deposit interdigital

A magnificent white-tailed buck in autumn scenery.

The buck will trickle urine over his tarsal glands while rubbing the glands together in rub-urination.

scent on the ground. In one of their most complex scent-marking behaviors, deer deposit tarsal gland scent in scrapes through rub-urinating. Tarsal glands on the lower legs emit an oily secretion through the skin via ducts that lie along the hair follicles. Erector pili muscles along the hair let the hairs contract so tightly they resemble a shoe polish brush. The closed hairs minimize the gland's odor. When the deer is alarmed or aggressive, however, the erector pili muscles flare the tarsal hairs open like a rosette, maximizing surface area and scent dispersal.

When urinated on, tarsal glands' extruded lipids hold the urine, creating one of the whitetail's most powerful odors. In fact, under favorable conditions, even humans can smell a buck's tarsal glands at several hundred feet. Despite rub-urination's potency, even rutting whitetails often squat while urinating, preventing the urine from touching their tarsal glands. Likewise, although deer—especially dominant bucks—rub-urinate more often during the rut, deer of all ages and sexes rub-urinate throughout the year. In fact, I have videotaped a one-week-old fawn balance on teetering legs to rub-urinate.

Whitetails, blacktails, and mule deer rub-urinate. Elk have no tarsal glands but advertise their presence by frequently urinating on the long hair that hangs below their necks. Moose have small tarsal glands, but I have never seen them urinate on them. Rather, moose advertise by urinating in a muddy wallow, which they roll in to coat the flap of skin hanging beneath their necks. Caribou have large tarsal glands, but I have not seen them urinate on them.

What Triggers the Rut for Does?

Bucks come into rut before does enter estrus. In fact, bucks sometimes influence does to enter estrus earlier than normal. For example, does kept in research pens near rutting bucks often come into estrus several days earlier than normal because of the bucks' odor. I don't believe this happens in the wild, however, because non-estrous does avoid bucks to prevent harassment.

Photoperiodism triggers testosterone production in bucks and estrogen production in does. As a result, a doe's estrous period coincides with the latitude where she lives. For example, in northwestern New Jersey, the peak-rut occurs about November 9. On the other hand, John Ozoga has found the peak-rut in northern Michigan usually occurs about November 17. This regional difference ensures most fawn births coincide with the area's maximum vegetative output, which is necessary for fawn survival.

Photoperiodism is the amount of daylight within a twenty-four-hour period. Changes in day length cause a deer's pineal gland to signal the pituitary gland to increase or reduce the steroid hormone production of various organs. As day length decreases after June 21, melatonin production increases, causing a buck's testicles to enlarge, drop away from the body, and increase testosterone production. This triggers antler hardening and behavioral changes like rubbing and scraping. Increased melatonin production also causes a doe's ovaries to secrete more estrogen, prompting the doe to wean her fawns, accumulate fat, grow her winter coat, and eventually ovulate for breeding.

How Does Weather Affect Rut Activity?

Deer begin shedding their thin summer coats in mid-August, and by the end of September, their winter coat has replaced it. By mid-October, the new coat is completely grown in. The combination of heavy winter coats and high temperatures like those in 1998 kept deer movement to a minimum. Deer won't move until after the sun is down and the temperatures have dropped.

Doe-to-buck ratios also affect rut activity. In Pennsylvania, for example, far more adult bucks than does are killed each year, creating an adult doe-to-buck ratio of about 5-to-1 to 7-to-1. When there are far more does than bucks, rubbing and scraping activities are kept to a minimum because bucks have all the does they can breed.

Bucks gradually lose their red summer coats, which are replaced by gray winter hair by the middle of August.

With cold weather, deer will be more active; and more chasing will ensue. The extra chasing and the proximity and smell of the bucks might cause a doe to ovulate a day or two early, but that's it. Deer can't, and shouldn't, move their breeding period out of sync because it would affect the birthing period. Fawns are born mid-May to mid-June when food and weather conditions offer optimal survival rates.

Can Hunters Smell Rutting Bucks?

Some rutting bucks emit tremendous odors, and it's possible to smell a buck without seeing him. In fact, I have smelled hundreds of rutting bucks without seeing them. The odor of a buck in rut, produced primarily by the tarsal gland scent and urine, is so strong that almost any hunter can smell it. The strong odor is seasonal because the buck's tarsal glands are driven by testosterone. A dominant buck emits stronger odors than an immature buck, because a dominant buck urinates on his tarsal glands more frequently as the rut progresses.

During the Rut, I Saw Seventeen Scrapes in a 40-Yard Stretch—Is This Unusual?

Seventeen scrapes in such a small area is a lot of scrapes for any part of the country, and almost unheard of in the North. In both Texas and Alabama, I have seen scrape lines with a scrape every 50 to 75 feet. I just couldn't believe it when I first saw it in Alabama, but my friend, the late Ben Rogers Lee, said that was common in the South. On some Texas ranches, scrapes are even more plentiful.

I don't classify scrapes into categories, as many people do. First, bucks don't really have a territory, they have a home range. Their breeding area is where the most food is, because that's where the does will be.

A scrape is an advertisement of billboard proportions. In using scrapes made by other bucks, a buck can try to cancel out previous "messages" left by other bucks. This also allows bucks to monitor the presence of other competitors in the breeding chase. I guess you could say that scrapes are the closest thing to a singles bar that deer have. They literally reek "I'm here to take on all challengers."

This buck is rubbing scent from his forehead and preorbital glands on the overhead vine while on a scrape.

Is the Rut Different down South?

The rut in central Florida is about two months later than in Ohio. It should peak in mid-January. This makes the birth of the fawns, the peeling of velvet, and everything else connected to the deer's yearly cycle two months later than the timing of northern deer. The tiny deer of the Florida Keys might breed in any month of the year, as deer do in Central America; but of course, they can't be hunted.

The size of the deer in any locale is the result of Bergman's biological law, which states, "The farther north a species is found, the larger it will be." The species then has more body mass in comparison with exposed surface area as a heat-retention factor. Deer in Florida do not have to be as big as northern deer because they have access to growing vegetation on a year-round basis. They don't need to put on body fat, as they don't need insulation because it doesn't get cold.

Note the large preorbital gland in front of this buck's eye and the saliva bubble he is drooling.

A buck's scrape is a "billboard" to advertise his presence.

I don't have personal experience with deer in Florida, but I've seen more deer sign in Alabama, Louisiana, and Texas than I ever did up north. I base that on the fact that in my area of New Jersey, our mature buck ratio to mature does is 1-to-5 or 1-to-7. With those odds, our bucks don't need to advertise their presence as much as do bucks in the South, where the ratio is more likely to be 1-to-1 or 1-to-2. With those ratios the competition is higher and bucks make far more sign. I've watched bucks in Texas mark trees, rubs, and scrapes every 50 feet or so.

The same goes for rattling and grunting. Both procedures work far better in the South than they do in the North, and they do work in the North. In Texas, bucks almost run over you when you rattle antlers. In some areas, if you rattle a corn bucket, they will run over you. I can really offer no suggestions, other than to make sure you time your hunting activity to the deer's annual cycle.

CHAPTER 3

Interesting Behavior

I Saw a Deer Make Extra-High Jumps While Running—Is This Unusual?

I have seen deer make those high jumps just as you describe. Usually, about every fourth jump will be a high one. I once thought the extra-high jump was done as sort of an "observation" jump so the deer could better see over the high weeds. After years of observing both captive and wild deer where hunting is not allowed, however, I have concluded that high jumps are characteristic of individual deer.

For example, I photographed deer in one of our national parks long enough to get to know which deer was which by antler shape. Two bucks invariably made those high jumps on every fourth or fifth jump, and it didn't matter whether they were running across a field of high weeds or grazed-off pasture. When they ran, they jumped.

Do Does Use the Same Birthing Territory Year after Year?

The dominant doe in an area selects a birthing area with the best cover, food, and water. The subordinates take what's left, with first-time does being forced to take the least desirable territories.

Although some bucks make an occasional high jump when running to see over vegetation, others jump high habitually.

Although the doe chooses the area, the fawn selects its own bedding spot.

Because they do not always have safe territories, fawn mortality from first-time does is almost always higher than it is for the older, more experienced does. As older does die, younger does move up the hierarchy and claim better territories in succeeding years. When a doe has a good territory, she develops an affinity for it and will use the same territory until she dies, or until something changes that makes it less desirable.

For years, I watched a doe use a high piece of ground in a swampy area for her birthing territory. Even after she became old and was no longer the dominant doe in the area, she retained the rights to "her" territory. I know she used that territory for at least ten years.

My Doe-in-Heat Lure Attracted an Aggressive Doe. It Walked within 3 Feet of Me and Acted like a Buck— Is This Unusual?

You did not say what actions the doe took that were like a buck's, so I can only assume she acted aggressively with laid-back ears, raised hair, a stiff-legged walk, and so on. First of all, I have never

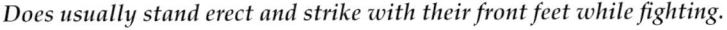

Does usually stand erect and strike with their front feet while fighting.

This buck is showing the extreme aggression commonly known as the "hard stare."

had a wild deer walk within 3 feet of me. That's most unusual. I have had them come within 5 to 6 feet, but never 3 feet.

Have I ever seen a doe act aggressively? Yes. I've seen the laid-back ears and the "hard stare" look, but I can't recall a doe causing all of her hair to stand on end aggressively. I imagine does can do so because they must have erector pili muscles, as I have seen their hair stand on end to increase the depth of insulation against the cold. I have never seen a doe use the stiff-legged walk that bucks commonly use in their threat gesture. Usually aggressive actions were against other does and bucks where food, such as dropped apples, was concerned.

I've seen adult does act aggressively against adult bucks during the rut when they were in a pre-estrous condition and were not yet ready to breed. It is common to see this type of aggression by adult does against related yearling bucks when they are chasing them out of their area, causing them to disperse. I've never seen a wild doe act aggressively toward a human. There's also the chance that the doe you saw acted the way she did because she had more of the male hormone, testosterone, than is normal.

Should I Avoid Taking Buck Fawns so I'll Have More Bucks Next Season?

The button bucks you see this fall will be next year's buck crop. In most states, yearling bucks make up 85 percent of the harvest. A doe will chase last year's fawns from her immediate birthing area, but she doesn't chase them far. Her birthing territory might be less than 1 acre in size. She will chase them from her home range when

When a buck fawn's pedicles begin to grow he is known as a "button" buck.

they are fifteen months old to prevent inbreeding. Most yearling bucks, however, move about 5 miles or so.

The main reason a doe first chases her last year's young away is to prevent them from being near and moving about when she gives birth to her new fawns. New fawns imprint and follow whatever moves in their area when they are born. With no other deer in the vicinity, the fawns imprint on just their mother's scent and voice. You wrote that you hunt 300 acres; there is little chance the button bucks you see this fall will be on your property next year.

I've Watched Enclosed Bucks Stare and Rub a Sapling but Not Fight—How Come?

An angry buck might well take out his frustration on a sapling. I've seen such actions countless times. I call it "replacement aggression." The bucks did not fight because, being inside an enclosure,

This buck is depositing forehead scent on the vine that he is rubbing.

they've probably fought before and each knew his place in the hierarchy. The fact they circled each other, as you wrote, means they are pretty evenly matched and will probably fight again if the lesser buck sees a sign of weakness in the more dominant buck. I'm willing to bet that the lesser buck was the one that beat up that sapling, taking out frustrations that he didn't dare unleash on the dominant buck. The dominant buck will be dominant only as long as he can maintain his strength. Some older dominant bucks become exhausted three-quarters of the way through the rut and simply walk away from all encounters. They might rest for a week and then fight their way back up the ladder, or they might retire for the rest of the season.

I once saw a small 6-point buck meet up with a big 8-point buck. There was never a chance for a fight, as there was too much size difference. When the big buck gave the little buck the hard stare, the 6 pointer hurried away. When the bucks were about 100 feet apart, they both started to vigorously rub saplings. It was as if the little buck was showing the big buck what he would like to do to him. In turn, the big buck was showing the little buck what he could do to him. It was a good example of replacement aggression.

Does Barometric Pressure Affect Deer Behavior?

Barometric pressure has much to do with deer movement. The barometer itself isn't a great forecaster, but a rising barometer going above 29.50 is usually an indication that good weather is on the way while a falling barometer presages a storm. When the barometer is falling, the wind usually blows in a counterclockwise direction, which in New York means that moisture will be brought in from the North Atlantic Ocean in the form of a nor'easter storm. With a rising barometer, the wind usually flows in a clockwise pattern, bringing drier air that has most likely passed over land.

I believe deer feel the difference in atmospheric pressure before most of our meteorological instruments detect it. Consequently, deer usually feed heavily before any kind of a storm but almost always before a protracted snowstorm. When you see deer feeding in open areas at midday, you can bet that a storm is on the way.

I don't think atmospheric pressure can be blamed for a lack of deer sightings—unless the barometer is dropping very rapidly. You

Only equal animals fight and do so to achieve dominance.

also mentioned that you had a full moon. My studies have shown that a full moon—particularly during the hunting season when there is a lot of pressure—causes deer to feed more often at night and, in turn, reduces their daytime activity.

What Causes Curled Toes?

Elongated toenails, although not common, are not a great rarity. This condition, which is also seen in cattle, is often referred to as "slipper foot." It is usually a chronic response to ingestion of a high-carbohydrate diet. Kerry Beheler, a wildlife health specialist at the Wisconsin Department of Natural Resources, reported that slipper foot cases have increased in her state, especially in areas where deer frequent feed/bait piles of corn. Under ordinary conditions, where the hoof makes contact with the ground, the hoof tip is constantly being worn down. When it does not contact the ground, it continues to grow.

The most extreme example I've ever seen were the hooves of a deer shot in New Jersey by one of my readers who was kind enough to send me a hoof for my collection. I have also seen this condition in wild sheep, elk, and other deer. An extreme example of elongated hooves are those of the lechwe, an African water antelope. To prevent this from happening in horses, blacksmiths trim horses' hooves when they shoe them. I do not believe this condition is painful for animals, although it does handicap them while walking by entangling them in vegetation.

Do Deer Get Frostbite?

I saw many exceptionally thin deer that died of starvation after the hard winter of 1960–1961 that were exceptionally thin but, even then, none of them exhibited any sign of frostbite. I suppose it could happen, but I've never seen it in person. *Deer & Deer Hunting*, however, has published several photos in the "Deer Browse" column over the years showing deer that have lost parts of their ears to frostbite.

Do Deer Urinate on Each Other's Urine, Like Dogs Do?

Dogs are territorial, as are foxes, coyotes, and wolves, and they all mark the periphery of their territory with urine and feces as a way of making those boundaries known to other members of their own species. A dog, by urinating on tires, is merely reclaiming the car as part of his territory by nullifying the rival dogs' urine. Deer are not territorial, except for does defending their birthing territories, but they employ their urine exactly as dogs do to announce their presence and assert their hierarchical status.

The scent of each animal is unique, and all deer know the scent of every other deer in their home territories. Upon recognizing another deer by the scent of its urine, a deer knows what its status is; because all deer in the same area have tested themselves against every other deer. Fights between bucks usually occur only when a rival buck from another area tests himself against the dominant buck on his home turf, or when a young buck, reaching his prime, tries to replace an older buck that had previously dominated him.

It is well-known that bucks urinate in the scrapes they make, and I consider scrapes as the deer "billboard" of communication. There is ample sign for all to see, and urine to smell. What is lesser known is the frequency with which bucks urinate on top of the

A major scrape usually has an overhanging branch the buck can rub and chew on. This scrape has been used traditionally for many years.

urine from other deer away from scrapes. There are no signs to be seen after the urine has dried, and I know deer do this only because I have spent thousands of hours watching and studying deer over my lifetime. I have also noticed that bucks urinate on top of almost every doe's urine, but they also urinate on top of some other bucks' urine. Animals live in a world of scent, and unfortunately, we humans do to a far lesser extent, so we can only guess at what goes on in the world around us unless we actually see it.

Do Deer's White Eye Rings Change?
No, the white ring around a deer's eye stays the same in size and color throughout the year. The deer's summer coat varies from a deep russet-red to a sandy tan, and against those lighter colors, the white eye ring doesn't show as prominently. When deer are in their dark winter coats, the eye ring is much more conspicuous.

Do Does Drip from the Mouth?
I've never seen a doe drip from the mouth, and I don't believe they do because the dripping is caused by the influence of the male sex hormone, testosterone. Bucks usually start to drip around September 1, and the amount of moisture that is dripped increases all through the rutting season before tapering off and finally stopping during the latter part of December.

Have You Ever Seen a Deer Challenge a Horse?
Having been raised on a farm in the 1930s, when we used horses for work, I am familiar with their relationship with deer. Deer usually avoid close contact with horses and cattle. I don't, however, think deer fear them. When deer feed in the same field as cattle and horses, they just get out of the way if the livestock approach.

In fact, I used to get close to deer by riding my horse among them. To further conceal my presence, I would ride bareback and lie on the horse's back. Evidently, the deer didn't see or smell me. I have never seen a buck challenge a horse, as you said you have. Your encounter was especially unusual because the horse must have been several times larger than the buck, and virtually all wild creatures respect larger animals. I assume the bizarre behavior stemmed from rutting urges. Considering the challenge was brief, however, the young buck you saw must not have lost all of his marbles.

Will Nose Bots Affect Meat Quality?

According to the Southeastern Cooperative Wildlife Disease Study Group, nasal bots have never harmed anyone. Undoubtedly, something else was wrong with the deer you described as being two and a half years old and only weighing 108 pounds. You were wise not to eat the meat if it had anything other than a normal appearance or gave off an odor. I don't know what was wrong with the deer, but it was not caused by nasal bots.

I urge readers to notify their game or health officers if they encounter any deer that does not appear to be healthy. With West Nile virus, chronic wasting disease, and epizootic hemorrhagic diseases spreading, we all have to be on the alert.

Will Cutting Down Rubs Stimulate Activity?

Cutting down buck rubs will have no effect on buck activity. When bucks are only moving at night, it indicates heavy hunting pressure. Heavy hunting pressure might cause bucks to become strictly nocturnal, even if the rut's in full swing. Cutting down the rubs will not alter this behavior; and even leaving a lot of human scent in the area of the rubs will only reinforce the bucks' decision not to move.

Although bucks rub throughout the rut, they actually make more rubs during the pre-rut. After the pre-rut or even after most of the rut is over, bucks have a diminished interest in rubs.

Are Buck and Doe Droppings Different?

No, the shape and consistency of deer pellets has nothing to do with the deer's sex. It has everything to do with the moisture content of various foods. When deer feed on succulent grasses in spring, and especially when they eat fruits and berries, their feces have the consistency of cow flops—there are no pellets. The main difference is a cow flop is formless, being looser. Normal deer feces are about 1½ inches in diameter and 3 to 6 inches in length; being loose, they are not perfectly round, but flattened into those dimensions.

In early autumn, when deer eat acorns, corn, and freshly fallen leaves, the pellets might sometimes be clumped together because there's some moisture in those foods. In late fall and winter, however, pellets are almost always individualized because deer mainly feed on dry leaves, dried vegetation, and browse. Because of the increased rough fiber in their diet, the pellets will also be much darker, compressed into individual pellets; and while some will be tapered on both ends, some will be tapered on one end and indented on the other where they were impressed upon each other as they passed through the intestines. My research shows that large pellets are usually from large deer, while small pellets are from young deer.

I Killed an 8-Point Buck That Didn't Have a Penis or Testicles—Have You Ever Heard of This?

Yes, several people have written to me over the years stating they have encountered the same situation. It is not a common occurrence, however, and I have not seen it myself. You did not mention if your deer also had a vagina. I believe your deer was probably a hermaphrodite, having both male and female sex organs. Even without testicles, it evidently had enough testosterone in its system to produce hardened antlers. Having hardened antlers suggests the deer was more male than female and would not have been able to bear young. Deer bearing antlers that never harden, however, have been known to produce fawns.

What Are the Wet Spots I Found in a Deer Bed?

I have seen the spots you describe; and, in fact, I have actually seen captive deer make them. The spots were made where bedded deer were chewing their cud. Just like some people chew with their mouths open, so do some deer. I believe what you saw were puddles of saliva where deer drooled as they chewed. These types of puddles are commonly found near deer beds.

This buck is using his hind hoof to scratch an itch on his head.

Why Do Deer Chew Their Cuds Less Than Sheep Chew Theirs?

Deer are selective feeders and choose the most tender parts of the most desirable forage possible. Wild sheep and goats are more like cattle in that they eat more grasses than forbs. Usually, grasses are much more fibrous than forbs, which is why goats chew their cud about twice as long as deer. It takes much more chewing to break down grasses. No matter how soft a deer's food is, however, it still chews each mouthful about forty to forty-five times.

Chewing cud, in all ruminants, can be a voluntary and involuntary action. After filling its paunch, a deer finds a safe bedding area and begins to chew its cud. If it's disturbed or alarmed the deer will instantly stop chewing and swallow its cud. That's a voluntary action. Deer also chew their cud while they are sleeping, which is an involuntary action—the same as breathing.

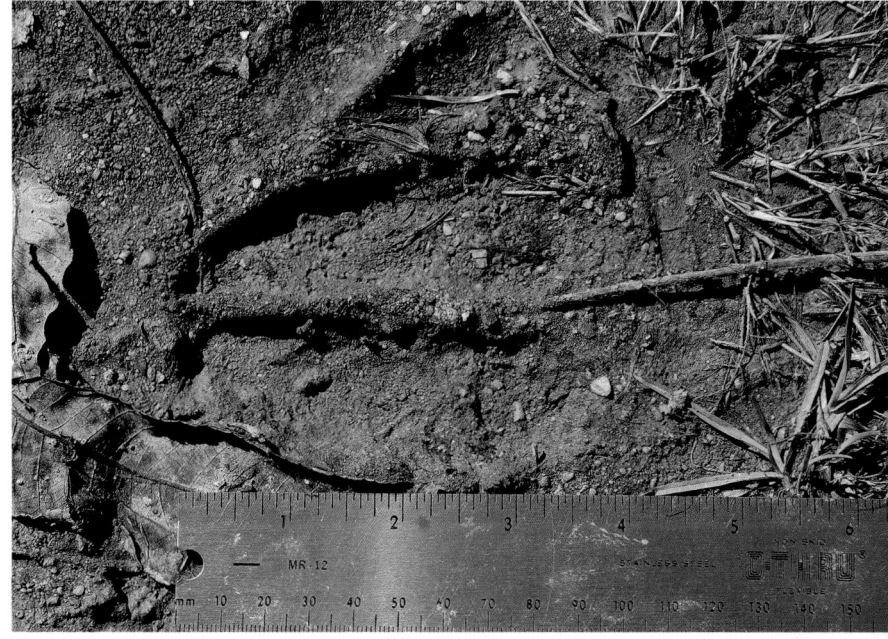

A deer track measuring 4 inches in length has to be made by a buck weighing more than 200 pounds.

Why Are a Deer's Front Hooves Larger Than Its Hind Hooves?

The front hooves of most cervids are about one-third larger than the hind hooves because most of these animals carry about one-third more weight on their front hooves. The haunches, or hams, are much larger than the shoulders because huge muscles are needed to power the animal when it runs and jumps. The large rear muscles are offset by the weight and size of the animal's long neck, head, and antlers. The moose is the most extreme example, as its body tapers from its huge antlers, neck, and high shoulders to much smaller hind parts. To carry that extra weight on its front legs, it needs larger hooves to provide a larger bearing surface. This prevents moose from sinking in the soft ground they often frequent.

Having more weight distributed on the forequarters provides the added advantage of more stability during fights. Most male

In a really vicious fight, one buck may be thrown off his feet occasionally.

members of the deer family have branched antlers they use to throw their opponents to the ground or push them backward. These fights involve much twisting and turning of the combatants' heads, necks, and bodies. To prevent being thrown, bucks use a wide stance with their front hooves and do most pushing with their heavily muscled hindquarters. Despite being muscular, however, hindquarters bear less weight than forequarters, making them easily moved. During a fight, a deer's hindquarters bounce all over. Deer would not be as agile if their hindquarters were heavier.

Not all animals share this characteristic. Rodents, for example, have larger hind feet because they have much heavier hindquarters. Rodents' hips are also higher than their shoulders because most of them bound when they run. This is also true of the weasel, raccoon, and bear families. Like deer, members of the cat and dog families carry most of their weight on their forequarters; and, therefore, have larger front feet.

A buck's growing antler is the fastest growing form of mammalian tissue, growing at a rate of a $^1/_4$ to $^1/_2$ inch per day.

Why Are Bucks Harder to See in the Summer?

During spring and summer, bucks' antlers are growing, making them soft and easily damaged. Broken or malformed antlers hamper a buck's dominance potential. To protect their antlers, bucks move no more than necessary. This is especially easy in summer because peak vegetative growth lets bucks fill their paunches with little time and effort. Therefore, bucks are not as active or visible during summer as during fall and winter.

Bucks also seem to be more affected by heat than does. Adult bucks are one-third to one-half larger than does and thus produce more body heat. A larger body is harder to cool, so bucks feed later than does on hot days. Therefore, you might be seeing fewer bucks because they are moving after nightfall.

Are Deer Afraid of Thunderstorms?

I don't believe wild creatures fear thunder and lightning. Those natural phenomena occur regularly; and because adult animals do not fear storms, juveniles do not acquire such fears. Although deer do not fear thunder and lightning, they do alter their behavior during thunderstorms. Normally, heavy rain accompanies a thunderstorm, and most animals try to avoid the short, heavy downpours by seeking shelter. Long rains, even if heavy at times, do not disturb wildlife as much; and most animals maintain normal activities.

Regardless of if they fear it, lightning occasionally kills deer and other wildlife. I know of three instances where deer were killed by lightning. In the one incident, deer were feeding near a barbwire fence when lightning struck the wire. The charge presumably jumped to the deer, killing them. Strangely, there were no marks on the deer. In another instance, a buck had been feeding on an open, grassy hilltop when he was struck by lightning. There was no doubt what had happened because the buck had a streak of singed hair running from his back down his leg.

Does Black Bear Predation Affect Deer Populations?

I believe bear predation on all types of wildlife is heavier than generally acknowledged, mostly because few people witness it. In Alaska's Denali National Park, for example, up to 80 percent of moose calves are killed by grizzly bears annually. I have also seen bears ambush and kill bull caribou. According to Denali park biologists, 77 percent of caribou calves born in the park in 2001 were killed by bears and wolves by July l.

Of course, bears also affect wildlife in the continental United States. For example, I recently spoke to photographers who had witnessed grizzlies killing newborn bison in Yellowstone National Park. One photographer even saw a grizzly grab a protruding calf from a birthing bison cow, killing the calf before it hit the ground.

My area in New Jersey has also seen a dramatic increase in black bear populations. In fact, bear numbers have become so high they have affected my captive whitetail operation. My pen is inhabited by 5 white-tailed does. Although those does usually have 10 fawns each year, they had only 4 in Summer 2001. That year, a black bear often raided my pen for its high-protein deer feed. One day, my secretary saw the bear run off with a fawn in its mouth. Considering these examples, I think a large black bear population can negatively affect the deer herd. Both animals frequent the same habitat, and bears are constantly searching for food. I don't doubt black bears hunt white-tailed fawns as diligently as grizzlies hunt moose calves.

All bears are omnivorous—their teeth show that. They have the long, curved canine teeth to grasp their prey, and flat-topped molars for grinding vegetation, which makes up most of their diet. In short, they are opportunists and eat almost anything they can find or capture, including adult deer.

I know a hunter who recently arrowed a big, droop-eared buck. I had seen the buck previously and had attributed the drooped ear to an injury suffered while battling another buck. I learned otherwise, however, when my friend's taxidermist reported that he hit something hard in the cartilage at the base of the buck's ear while caping out the head. Closer examination disclosed a large black bear claw. Evidently, a bear had attacked the buck, or—perhaps in defense—the buck had attacked the bear. Regardless, the bear must have swatted the buck's head and lost a claw in the process. The deer lost control of his ear, but both animals survived. That's an encounter I would have loved to have seen!

What Do Deer Tail Movements Indicate?

Yes, there is a "tail language." White-tailed deer often unintentionally telegraph their intentions through their tails. Mule deer and blacktails, however, don't. A feeding whitetail almost always wags its tail before raising its head. If you are stalking a deer, freeze when you see the tail wag and don't move until the head goes down again.

A deer holding its tail out horizontally usually smells something of interest. A buck walking with his head down and tail pointing straight out is probably tracking a pre-estrous doe or perhaps another buck. A deer that holds its tail straight up with the hairs compressed is probably defecating. If you are close, you can see the pellets drop, but you probably won't notice this from a distance.

This buck is displaying the flared, white tail from which his species gets its name.

When deer are alarmed, they flare their tails. Large deer can flare their tails to a width of 11 inches. When the tail is raised vertically; this is especially noticeable because, if the deer is facing away from you, the large white tail and the exposed white rump hairs make a white patch 1 foot wide by about 3 feet high. Pronghorn antelope exhibit similar behavior. In fact, they are often called "heliographers"; because by raising and lowering their rump rosette, they can send visual danger signals to other antelope a mile or more away. Reflected light from a whitetail's rump hair and flared tail are visible from at least a quarter mile.

When does run, they almost always raise their tails, flare them widely, and let them flop loosely from side to side. They do this to serve as a beacon to their fawns in low light. Some bucks raise and flare their tails while running. Heavily hunted bucks usually clamp their tails down, however, presumably because raising their tails attracts attention, which is the last thing they want when trying to leave an area undetected. In cold weather, most deer keep their tails clamped down to conserve body heat.

Do Deer Use Migration Routes?

I can assure you that some deer follow traditional wintering routes. George Shiras III told of deer migrating in the 1890s. I also realize that because Michigan's Upper Peninsula has been heavily logged, not as many deer now migrate, nor do they travel as far.

Most migrations are triggered by photoperiodism—the number of daylight hours in a twenty-four-hour period. As the days get shorter in autumn, the pineal gland receives less light; and when a certain stage is reached, birds head south and animals migrate. But animals don't necessarily head south. In New York's Adirondack Mountains, some deer migrate north to the lowland conifer areas where they yard for the winter.

Weather also has a lot to do with migration. In Wyoming, most folks pray for an early snowstorm because that sends elk and mule deer streaming from the mountains to the valleys. Usually, females migrate first, governed by photoperiodism, but it's snow that pushes the males down.

There's great controversy over whether migration routes are instinctual or learned. I believe that most animal migration routes, particularly shorter routes (50 to 100 miles) to specific areas are taught to the younger animals by adults. I also know that some of the long, general-area migrations of birds are done by instinct because in some cases, the immature birds go south for their first winter while the adults stay north.

How Old Does an Average Deer Get?

Unhunted deer have an average life expectancy of twelve and a half years. Of course, most wild deer do not reach that age. In heavily hunted areas, most bucks are killed at age one and a half. Even in protected refuges and national parks where deer eat just natural browse and vegetation, they seldom live longer than twelve years

The entire posture and flared tail of this young button buck shows he is extremely alert.

because by the time they reach that age, their molars are worn to the gumline. Without good teeth, even if food is plentiful, deer cannot get all of the nutrition that is in the food because they can't chew it properly. Deer in captivity, which are fed softer foods, can live much longer, despite the condition of their teeth. In the wild in the South, however, where the weather is warmer and more natural soft food is available for much of the year; deer can live longer.

I have a jawbone from one of my captive does that lived seventeen and a half years. My friend Joe Taylor had a captive doe that lived to be twenty years, seven months. My friend Ben Lingle had a captive buck that lived to be twenty years, ten months. Two out-

At the first indication of danger, this buck dashes off into cover.

Adult bucks have a much heavier body and a deeper chest depth than younger deer.

standing longevity records were reported in *Outdoor Alabama* in 1984. A doe that had been tagged and stocked as a juvenile was shot in 1981, when she was twenty-one years old. Even more remarkable, an adult doe was tagged and stocked in 1961 and was shot in 1983. This doe had to be at least twenty-three years old. Neither doe strayed beyond the area where it was stocked. It makes one wonder just how much longer they might have lived if they had not been killed by hunters. Would these does have been able to survive so long in the North amid extreme cold and short rations? We will never know, but we do know that they lived longer than any other wild whitetails on record.

Do Does Bleed when Breeding?

No, does do not discharge vaginal blood in their urine before, during, or after breeding. Members of the canine family bleed prior to and during their estrous period; and because many hunters are familiar with this, they assume that deer do, too. Members of the cervid family do not bleed. Doe urine does turn orange after deer yard up. This is not because blood is mixed with urine, but because the deer are on a restricted food intake and are metabolizing their body fat.

Do Doe Fawns Breed?

Most doe fawns do not breed. A doe fawn must weigh about 80 pounds in order to breed. Few doe fawns reach that weight by December, especially in the North. About 40 percent of New Jersey's doe fawns reach that weight and breed while about 80 percent of the doe fawns in Indiana and Illinois reach the required weight. This is all based on the amount of available food. In the North, most adult does breed in November, and most doe fawns breed in December.

Do Deer Sleep with Their Eyes Open?

I believe deer typically sleep with their eyes open. Deer sleep only seconds to minutes at a time, and even when asleep, they swivel their ears constantly. Deer sometimes sleep with their eyes closed, but usually keep them at least partially open. Deer sleeping with their eyes open, however, aren't alert if there is no disturbing noise.

Ordinarily, a deer sleeps with its head upright, although its head usually lowers as the animal drifts into deeper sleep. Deer are rarely exhausted or confident enough to place their heads on the ground while sleeping. To curl its head back over its body a deer must feel secure.

A few years ago, while concealed in a blind, I videotaped a doe, dominant buck, and three subordinate bucks—exhausted from chasing—rest their heads on the ground and sleep. The dominant buck's eyes were closed, while the doe's eyes were partially open. I could not see the subordinate bucks' eyes. Although the deer were clearly exhausted, none slept more than a minute or two. After waking, they scanned their surroundings, then seeing nothing dangerous, drifted back to sleep.

Deer seldom rest their head on the ground except during the rutting season when they are physically exhausted. They often sleep with their eyes open.

I Saw a Deer with White Clumps and Strips of Grass Hanging off Its Belly—What's the Explanation?

The growths were probably infectious cutaneous fibromas. Cutaneous fibromas, however, usually have gray, warty exteriors. I have seen the skin split on some large fibromas, revealing a white interior, which you might have seen. As for the grass, I suspect the doe had tumors on its chest or belly. These tumors might have rubbed raw while the doe bedded, allowing grass to adhere to them. The grass was still green because the doe was probably bedded moments before passing your stand.

Before Giving Birth, Do Does Drive off Yearlings?

Just before giving birth, does drive off their previous year's fawns, which are then yearlings. A doe defends its birthing territory from other deer to prevent its fawns from imprinting on other deer. Does maintain this exclusive birthing territory for about three weeks until the fawns are large and strong enough to follow them. Does then give up their birthing territory and join matriarchal groups. At that time, yearling does rejoin their mothers. About 50 percent of yearling bucks driven from their mothers home ranges disperse at that time.

Telemetry studies on radio-collared deer have shown yearling bucks disperse 5 miles on average. Forty percent to 50 percent of yearling bucks rejoin the matriarchal group and will be chased away by their mothers and other adult does before the rut, usually in late September. This almost eliminates inbreeding; because most bucks disperse five miles, taking them beyond their mothers' home ranges. Incidentally, because of these dispersal patterns, vehicle-deer collisions increase dramatically in spring and fall.

One Summer, I Saw a Deer Lying Down with Its Front Legs Extended Forward—Was It Hurt?

In cold weather, deer and other ungulates lie with their hooves tucked under their bodies. This keeps the animal's legs warm and prevents complete compression of belly hair. A deer's winter hair provides excellent insulation. To increase this benefit, a deer's hair often stands on end so that more dead air is trapped in between

In cold weather all deer like to bask in the sunlight on southern-sided hilltops.

each hair. Trapped air provides excellent insulation, which is why birds fluff out their feathers in cold weather.

When a deer beds in snow, its body weight compresses most of the air out of the hair, resulting in heat loss. By folding its legs beneath its body, however, not all of the deer's body touches the snow, allowing increased heat retention. The doe you saw most likely had its legs outstretched for the opposite reason. By having its legs outstretched the blood flowing through the deer's legs could cool quickly, thus regulating the deer's temperature in warm weather. Having more of its body in contact with the cool, damp ground quite likely helped cool the doe.

Deer frequently bed in front of rocks or logs during cold weather to be warmed by the reflected sun.

Fawns depend on their spotted coats to escape detection during the first weeks of their lives.

Why Would a Buck Have Spots?

Out of the countless deer I have seen, only about twelve retained vestiges of their spotted fawn coats as adults. The spots are light brown, making them almost invisible at a distance. These spots get fainter as the deer ages. If the buck is a yearling, the spots are most likely quite prominent. I don't know why some deer retain their spots. Such markings typically consist of two plain spinal rows with a few spots in between. The spots usually aren't on the deer's sides and legs.

What's a "Licking Stick"?

A licking stick is a 1-inch-diameter sapling a buck has broken off about 30 inches above the ground. Occasionally, deer use dead saplings or upturned root snags for licking sticks, but these usually break too easily. Bucks seem to prefer more resilient sticks. Bucks rub their forehead scent glands on the stick, but do the most vigorous rubbing on the glands behind their antlers and in front of their ears. Bucks often alternate the rubbing, going behind the right antler, then behind the left, and then repeating the process. Bucks rub thirty to forty seconds, and then lick the stick. Rub-lick sequences last about five minutes.

Licking sticks offer excellent hunting, because like rubs and scrapes, licking sticks usually attract every deer that passes. They are hard to find, however, because they don't feature scrapes, and are usually found away from trails, scattered along oak ridges. A licking stick's only visible characteristic is that its bark will have been scraped off the top 8 inches.

I Killed a Deer That Had Three Warts—Can I Eat the Meat?
The venison is safe to eat. The warts were most likely cutaneous fibromas or papillomas caused by a viral infection spread by biting flies and midges. The virus affects only the deer's skin, and is harmless to humans.

Fibromas vary tremendously. For example, I have seen softball-sized fibromas and others that were elongated like a sausage. Unless the fibromas become large, or affect the deer's eyesight, they don't harm deer. In fact, I have seen seemingly healthy deer covered with thirty to forty fibromas. Fibromas freeze off in cold weather, and then heal over. Interestingly, a deer herd infected with fibromas one year might not be affected the next year.

Does Inbreeding Cause Spike Bucks?
Deer inbreeding is rarely a problem. In New Jersey, for example, almost 80 percent of bucks are killed each year, lowering the chances that a buck will reach sexual maturity in time to breed its female relatives. Inbreeding is also reduced by yearling buck dispersal. At age fourteen or fifteen months, most bucks leave their birth range voluntarily or are driven out by female relatives.

Spike bucks are common in areas with high deer populations because the habitat is holding more deer than it can support. They also result from late fawn births, which are common on overpopulated deer range. These late-born bucks struggle to attain proper nutrition and thus grow underdeveloped racks as yearlings.

This young buck has spikes, which are most often the result of inferior food, not bad genetics.

Spike bucks are not inbred or genetically inferior, as often thought. In fact, studies have proven that with age and proper nutrition, some spike bucks can grow record-class racks. Therefore, landowners are best served to kill more does and let spikes walk. This lets spikes reach maturity and allows the habitat to produce better forage.

Why Would a Buck Have Yellow Fat?

In the October 2001 edition of "Rue's Views," I struggled to explain why the buck an Iowa hunter had killed had yellow fat. Since that issue hit newsstands, I've received some expert insights about fat coloration in whitetails. Take, for example, comments from deer biologist Dwayne R. Etter of Urbana, Illinois. "I was a deer researcher/manager for the Chicago region from 1994 to 1998," Etter wrote. "In that time, I inspected thousands of deer culled by sharpshooters from December through March. Fat on those deer varied from white to yellow to red. Fat coloration appeared to vary between the sexes and in relation to the deer's fat levels. Older bucks typically had more yellowish fat than yearling bucks, whose fat was usually white. Fawns of both sexes typically had yellow fat later in the season. According to T. P. Kistner, deer fat is white during deposition and turns yellow or red as it's metabolized. Considering this, I suspect that because most hunters—particularly Northerners—rarely kill deer in late winter, they probably don't see fat being metabolized, which explains why most hunters have only seen white fat. If metabolism is related to coloration, older bucks' fat should be first to change from white to yellow, because they are metabolizing fat during the rut. When I made these observations, we were culling deer from populations that had been unhunted for thirty to forty years. Therefore, older bucks were common. As a result, yearling bucks rarely bred, which might explain why their fat was typically white. Fawns were next to metabolize fat as winter progressed. Red fat was common in emaciated animals, probably because such deer were metabolizing their little remaining fat."

I am embarrassed that I didn't think of this, because I have been gauging deer health by their bone-marrow fat color for years. I have written about marrow color change several times and I have talked about it in lectures. I never associated it, however, with changing color in body fat because I had never seen it. Of the hundreds of deer I've killed in October, November, and early December, all had white fat. I've killed most of my bucks, however, from late November to early December—usually the peak of the rut in my area—and their fat was white, so I doubt metabolism alone governs color change. I agree that fat metabolism during food shortages affects fat color. I have culled penned deer in late March and their fat was still white. They weren't stressed, however, by food shortages like free-ranging Northern deer.

A dairy cattle veterinarian from Royalton, Minnesota, offered a different explanation. "Last fall, a friend called me to examine a doe he was butchering that had yellow fat," the veterinarian wrote.

"This condition is called 'icterus,' or jaundice. In addition to yellow fat, the deer had a small liver for an animal its size. Considering this, I advised against eating the animal. Jaundice can develop in several ways. Molds, diseases, toxic plants or chemicals, and infectious diseases can affect the blood or liver and lead to jaundice. Overweight cattle subjected to infection or external stress are particularly susceptible to jaundice with liver disease. Often, they develop the jaundice with normal to excess fat still in their bodies. Minnesota whitetails experience many of these conditions in the form of liver flukes, clostridial diseases, moldy corn—specifically aflatoxin, infectious diseases like lepto and anaplasmosis, and foods like wild onion and rape," the veterinarian added. "Rape, for example, occasionally causes icterus or jaundice in cattle and is in many food-plot seed blends. Considering this, an overweight buck that gains breeding rights, is harassed by another rutting buck, or is driven from its home range and preferred food source could develop liver problems and discolored fat just like overweight dairy cattle."

While Butchering, I Discovered What Looked like Grubs in a Deer's Esophagus—What Were They?

I think the parasites you found were nasal botfly larvae. About five types of botflies infest deer, elk, moose, and caribou. After hatching from the larval stage, the adult flies breed. After breeding, female flies seek out a host animal on which to lay their eggs—often on a deer's nose. You might have witnessed this without knowing what you were seeing.

When the flies are trying to lay their eggs, deer frequently run a short distance and then stand with their noses practically touching the ground. If the flies persist, deer run, stop, and again put their nose to the ground. I have even seen deer paw at their nose with their hoof or rub their nose against their front leg to deter the flies.

After the flies lay their eggs, host deer inadvertently ingest the eggs when they lick their nose—which deer do constantly to keep nose tissues moist and increase their ability to trap scent particles. When these ingested larvae hatch, they migrate to the deer's nasal passage or lodge in the esophagus, as in the case of your buck. The larvae mature again, at which time they are coughed or sneezed out. The larvae then burrow into the ground and soon emerge as adult flies. Although a heavy botfly infestation might be an incredible nuisance and cause a deer to lose weight, most parasitologists believe botflies don't pose a health hazard to deer. Experts also believe a botfly-infected deer's meat is safe to eat, as botflies pose no health risks to humans.

Are Some Deer Nocturnal?

Deer are crepuscular, meaning they are most active in late afternoon and early morning. As hunting pressure increases, however, deer feed less in daylight and become nocturnal until about two weeks after hunting season. Deer then return to morning and afternoon feeding patterns. Incidentally, I believe most old bucks become strictly nocturnal throughout hunting season, even during peak-rut.

Can Antlered Does Breed?

Biologists have devoted much research to antlered does. At one time, Pennsylvania biologists estimated one out of every 18,000 antlered deer was actually a doe. As more states conducted such research, the antlered doe ratio was estimated as even higher. For example, New York researcher C. W. Severinghaus found his state produced about one antlered doe per 2,500 to 2,700 antlered bucks. In 1959, J. Kenneth Doutt and John C. Donaldson, of Pittsburgh's Carnegie Museum, found that of 38,270 antlered deer killed, 17 were antlered does, producing a ratio of 1-to-2,250—similar to New York's figures. Doutt and Donaldson continued their studies in 1961, reporting that out of 173,038 antlered deer killed in Pennsylvania within the previous four years, 43 were does—a ratio of 1-to-4,024. In the Pennsylvania study, no single area produced significantly more of these deer. Rather, the antlered does seemed randomly scattered throughout the state.

Antlered does fall into three categories. In the most common of the three, the antlers never harden, nor does the velvet peel. These antlers usually freeze and fall off during winter. Such does can breed and produce milk, as evidenced in 1967, when researchers discovered a four-year-old doe near Mercer, Pennsylvania. The doe, which was carrying triplets, was starting to grow a new set of antlers. Although such deer are technically female, they don't produce enough female hormones to suppress the somatotropic growth hormones of the pituitary glands. The antlers are formed under the stimulation of the pituitary. Because these does lack testicles, however, they don't produce enough testosterone to harden the antler and complete the cycle. In addition, their necks don't swell, nor do their hock hairs stain as darkly as a rutting buck's.

The second type of antlered doe is a buck with abnormal sex organs. These deer usually have a penis and a vagina, but the scrotum is not visible because the testicles are internal. Because they are not actually female, these deer never bear young. The antlers are like a typical buck's, often well-developed and polished. These bucks' necks don't become swollen during the rut.

The third condition is rare. It occurs when a tumor in the doe secretes male hormones. Male and female reproductive organs might be present, the antlers might not develop completely, and the rack often remains in velvet. As far as male behavior is concerned, none of these "does" has enough testosterone to be a complete, functioning male. I have not read of anyone seeing such deer acting aggressively or making a scrape. As for trying to breed another doe, a regular buck would probably prevent this. While growing up on my family's dairy farm, however, I noticed as cows entered estrus, some of the other cows mounted them. The same cows routinely did this, presumably because they had unusually high testosterone levels.

Also, antlers don't fall off while in velvet because they haven't completed their annual cycle. Several factors make bucks shed velvet late, but damage to their testicles is the most common reason. If severe, such an injury might prevent the antler from hardening. The rack would then probably freeze off during winter and wouldn't grow back the following year.

Do Coyotes Run off Deer?

No, coyotes do not chase deer off their home ranges. This past fall, I was photographing several deer from a blind when they stopped feeding and ran away. A coyote soon appeared and smelled where the deer had been but made no attempt to follow their trails. After investigating the area for a few minutes, it trotted out of sight. The deer didn't leave their home range, they just got out of the coyote's way.

I Once Saw a Deer That Seemed Unafraid Even When I Waved My Arms. I Walked Up to It and Saw That It Was Moving Its Front Legs but Not Its Back Legs. I Couldn't See Any Wounds. Any Explanation?

I think the deer was somehow crippled. I believe an accident had injured the spinal column, severing the nerve to the hind legs. I have seen several deer with similar injuries. Ordinarily, no wild animal that sees you will let you disappear from its sight. Even when we aren't hunting, wildlife perceive us as predators. When you disappear from view, deer figure you are stalking them and flee. The fact that a deer stays in the same spot and lets you approach it proves the severity of its handicap.

I also believe the accident was recent. If it had occurred long before the deer was shot, the hairs would have been rubbed off the top of its hind hooves because of being dragged. Considering the ground and vegetation were not worn down or overbrowsed, according to your account, I believe the deer had recently arrived on the scene. The lack of blood and puncture wounds indicates that the deer had been hit by an automobile and suffered spinal injuries that caused no external bleeding.

Despite the fact the deer was 2 miles from the nearest road, I still think an automobile was the culprit. I have seen many examples of deer traveling long distances after suffering severe injuries. For example, when I was a deputy game warden, I received a report that a young deer had been hit by a car. When I arrived at the scene about thirty minutes later, the deer was gone. The collision had injured the deer's spine, and the deer had dragged itself away. Despite the severity of its injuries, the deer had already traveled about a half mile and was moving at a good clip when I caught up with it and killed it. The deer could only move its front legs and was dragging the rear portion of its body and hind legs. You say you saw your deer about 10 A.M. If it had been struck by a car the previous evening at about 8 or 9 P.M.—a prime time for deer movement—it would have had thirteen to fourteen hours to pull itself up that mountain.

Can Whitetails and Mule Deers Interbreed?

Whitetails and muleys often interbreed. In fact, in western Texas, biologists are concerned whitetails will breed the desert mule deer out of existence. This has been caused by the proliferation of whitetails and crossbreeding. Although some biologists claim the offspring of whitetail–mule deer breeding are infertile, this is not necessarily true. These offspring are sometimes handicapped, however, because they cannot run from predators as effectively as their parents. I have not seen this, but I've heard these hybrids don't gallop as well as whitetails, nor stott as well as mule deer. When a doe of either species enters estrus, she attracts both species of bucks. Mule deer bucks, however, are not as persistent in chasing as are whitetails.

Why Would Some Deer Have Canine Teeth?

I have never seen canine teeth in a white-tailed deer, but that's not unusual, because these teeth are even more uncommon in northern deer. An adult deer has 32 teeth. Deer have no front upper teeth, but have 6 premolars and 6 molars, 3 of each on each side. The lower jaw has 6 incisors, 2 modified canines, 6 premolars and 6 molars—a total of 20 teeth—10 on each side.

Deer canines are not like meat-piercing canines of the dog family. In fact, a deer's canines so closely resemble its incisor teeth they are often classified and counted as such. In rare instances, deer have maxillary canine teeth in their upper jaw. These rudimentary canines serve no purpose because there are no opposing teeth. These teeth rarely erupt through the gums, and most people would be unaware of their presence.

Biologists locate unruptured canines by scraping the upper jaw. Noted deer researcher C. W. Severinghaus found only 23 upper canine teeth in 18,000 white-tailed deer he examined, or 0.1 percent. The farther south one goes, the higher the frequency of canine teeth in deer. Charles M. Loveless and Richard F. Harlow found 4 canine teeth in an examination of 95 deer in Florida, or 4.2 percent. At the Wilder Wildlife Refuge in Texas, 162 whitetail skulls yielded 49 canine teeth in 29 of the animals. Some of the skulls had only 1 canine, while others had 2. Twenty-six of the teeth were rudimentary and did not protrude through the gums. Among does, 18 percent had upper canines. Among bucks, 17 percent had them. In Venezuela, E. Boelioni found 4 large canine teeth in 10 deer he examined, or 40 percent.

The musk deer and the Chinese water deer have greatly elongated, functional, stabbing, maxillary canine teeth—tusks—and no antlers. The muntjacs, or "barking" deer, of southeast Asia have tusks and antlers. Biologists believe the canine teeth diminished in prehistoric deer with the evolution of antlers. Other members of the deer family, such as elk and caribou, also have canine teeth. Elk usually have well-developed maxillary canines.

For How Long Do Fawns Nurse?

Does nurse their fawns about four times, and no more than six times, in a twenty-four hour period. Newborn fawns nurse for the longest periods—about six to eight minutes. It is not that they are drinking more milk, it is just that it takes them longer to consume it.

Does wash their newborn fawns frequently as part of the bonding process.

Fawns also nurse longer because does stimulate their bowels by licking their anal region and consuming any feces and urine to keep the fawns and the area odor-free. This prevents predators from finding the fawns.

At one month, fawns nurse about five minutes at a time. By age six weeks to two months, they are being weaned and most nursing periods last only one to two minutes. By the time a fawn is one month old the doe is no longer consuming the feces and urine because the fawn can outrun most predators.

At five days of age a fawn can easily outrun a person.

Will the Button Bucks I See in Winter Have Antlers in the Fall?

Buck fawns will not develop antlers over winter. Buttons are caused by the formation of antler pedicles that will be the base from which all future antlers grow. These pedicles are long protrusions growing out of the frontal skull plate.

Occasionally, in areas of food with exceptionally high levels of protein, buck fawns develop antler nubs that protrude through the skin and hair. The nubs will be visible in December. A deer's metabolism, however, soon slows and antler growth stops. These nubs are shed in late winter, and the pedicles will be covered with new skin. This skin allows new antler growth in late March or early April.

Where Do Supplying Bloodlines Come from in Decimated Regions?

Any area can grow trophy deer, provided they live long enough to reach their potential. In New Jersey, about 86 percent of bucks are killed when they are one and a half years old. A yearling buck on a diet of at least 16 percent protein can grow an 8-point rack with $5/8$-inch diameter antler beams.

So much of New Jersey is being developed that deer hunting has become impossible in many areas. The destruction of habitat has greatly reduced the deer population and has displaced many deer. Numerous deer living between housing developments, however, are never hunted. Because such areas allow bucks to reach maturity, they are producing tremendous deer.

Are Whitetails Found in All Lower Forty-Eight States?

Few whitetails are found in California and Nevada, but I think they will expand their range there in the years to come. Years ago, when I guided wilderness canoe trips in Quebec, I saw whitetails expand their range northward about 100 miles in ten years. As Canadian International Paper logged spruce forests, cutover areas grew back quickly with birch, aspen, and berry bushes, providing excellent deer food. The loggers' presence also pushed wolves out of the area, and hunting pressure greatly reduced the moose population. As a result of fewer predators, less competition for browse, and moderate winters, the whitetail population exploded.

I have driven the Alcan Highway to Alaska twelve times since 1966. On each trip, I found whitetails farther north along the road. On the last trip in 2001, I saw whitetails just a few miles south of the Yukon Territory. If global warming continues, as it is predicted to, whitetails will soon pass that boundary as well.

Do Big Bucks Associate Only with Other Big Bucks?

No. After yearling bucks disperse, they usually join a group of other yearlings or mixed-age bucks. Yearlings, however, occasionally team up with a dominant buck. In fact, dominant bucks and yearlings often become inseparable, reinforcing their bond with mutual grooming, particularly around the head. Although the year-

Bucks stay together in a fraternal group and reinforce their bond in friendship by mutual grooming unless it's during the rutting season.

ling is always subordinate, the two bucks will spar often, which is important for the yearling's development. If the yearling doesn't build up his strength and sharpen his fighting skills, he will never work his way up the hierarchical ladder and become dominant.

How Many Generations Make Up a Matriarchal Group?

Research on captive and radio-collared does indicates matriarchal groups are usually composed of three generations of deer. Usually, when a doe is four years old, she leaves her family and becomes a matriarch. By that time, she should already have a family of her own. If deer are heavily hunted and older does are killed; family groups might not split up, leaving younger adult does to fill the void left by the death of the matriarch.

Group size is held down to three generations to minimize demand on the habitat. If a group's size increases, home-range size would have to increase for the group to find enough food. A white-tailed doe's home range remains fairly constant at 1 to 2 square

Deer live in a matriarchal society. Several family groups, however, may band together while feeding in the grasslands.

Sparring is only play-fighting, a time of testing.

miles. As forest-edge animals, deer hold their herd size down to stay in a smaller area they can get to know intimately. Although deer feed in large numbers while in open areas, they split up into their respective family groups when they return to cover.

Like most yearling bucks that move about 5 miles from their family area, some adult does disperse—although for shorter distances—when selecting birthing territories. As a result, they establish new home ranges. Their new home range might encompass a part of their old home range or might be beyond its boundaries.

Do Deer Play?

Starting when they're about four weeks old, fawns run, buck, jump, and kick with such vigor they sometimes fall down. By this time, matriarchal families have regrouped and fawns play frequently. Their play helps build muscle; increase lung capacity; strengthen the heart; and, in short, increase their survival chances.

The most intense play takes place on cool mornings and evenings. When the weather turns cooler in fall, does, yearlings, and even adult bucks participate in playtime activities including lots of play-fighting or sparring. A lot of the fawn play resembles children's games such as tag, running races, and hide-and-seek. All of these activities help deer build up the necessary strength to escape predators. Although play is an important part of fawn behavior and development, it requires calories. As a result, deer on an inadequate diet cannot afford the luxury of playing.

Do Older Bucks Have Higher Testosterone Levels?

Older bucks have much higher testosterone levels than those of younger bucks. In fact, research shows the presence of dominant

During the rutting season the bucks' necks bulk up because of the steroidal influence of the hormone testosterone.

bucks lowers the testosterone levels of young bucks. This helps prevent a chaotic breeding season. Dominance is communicated through testosterone transmitted through the forehead and tarsal glands. Hair on the forehead and tarsal glands of dominant bucks is typically much darker than that of subordinate bucks. Glands in the forehead give off an odor of their own, and fat from the sebaceous glands near the tarsal glands holds odors from the deer's urine placed there during rub-urination.

Why Do I See So Many More Does Than Bucks?

It's unusual for any area to have more bucks than does, even in unhunted areas. If you regularly walk your property, that might be your problem. Bucks are especially sensitive to disturbance in their core areas. To see more bucks, set up a blind downwind of a feeding area, and stay there until dark. Mature bucks are often the last deer to show up at a food source. In summer, bucks don't associate

Mature bucks court the does during the rutting season by grooming them.

After a fight, the victorious buck will chase the lesser buck out of the immediate area.

with does, although some might feed in the same area. In mid-September, bucks and does begin feeding together; and in mid-October, they are almost always together. Many deer disperse from their summer and early-fall range because there's little cover after crops are harvested.

Does Deer Dominance Change?

Dominance is constantly fluctuating. An animal is dominant only as long as it is bigger, stronger, and more aggressive than its counterparts. Lesser deer run off when the dominant doe shows up because she has most likely physically asserted her dominance over them. Does usually show dominance at food sources. That's why the dominant doe will accept social grooming when she is not feeding.

When Are Deer Ready to Reproduce?

Body weight has a lot to do with breeding ability. Research indicates that doe fawns are able to breed when they weigh 70 to 80 pounds. In highly fertile areas of the Midwest, about 60 percent of doe fawns breed when they are seven months old. This is also generally the case in the East, south of New Jersey. In the forests of northern New Jersey; northern Pennsylvania; the Adirondack region of New York; and most of New Hampshire, Vermont, and Maine, however, doe fawns typically don't reach that weight and do not breed until they are eighteen months old.

Most doe fawns do not breed until the first week of December, the so-called "second rut," because they need the additional month to gain the necessary weight. Most bucks cannot breed until they are eighteen months old. They occasionally, however, develop small antlers by January. If those antlers push through the skin and are polished, the buck fawn is able to breed. Although a buck fawn is large enough to breed a doe fawn, it would not be large enough to breed an adult doe. And if there was an adult buck nearby, it would not allow the buck fawn to be in the same area as an estrous doe.

Do Does Grunt?

Yes, does grunt. Does make low-pitched, short grunts to bring their fawns out of hiding for nursing.

Do Tarsal Glands Secrete?

The tarsal glands of bucks and does have sebaceous and sudoriferous glands. The sebaceous gland is more important to deer behavior, producing a fatty material along the tarsal-gland hairs. Deer urinate on these hairs and the urine adheres to this material. A bacteriological transformation caused by the reaction between the urine and sebaceous gland secretions produces the gland's dark stain and pungent odor. The more dominant the buck, the more frequently he urinates on his tarsal hairs and the darker the stain. Often, the stain runs down to the hooves. Because does urinate less often than bucks, their tarsal hairs do not become as dark or as potent-smelling as those of bucks. When I bowhunted, I cut off the tarsal glands of deer I killed, air-dried them, and used them as deer

The more dominant the buck the darker the urine-stained streaks going down his hind feet.

attractants. Between uses, I kept them in a sealed plastic bag, which helped retain the tarsal odor.

Bucks and does have scent glands on their foreheads, and they are major means of communication. Deer use them sparingly throughout the year; but during the rut, they become greatly enlarged in bucks and produce more secretions. Like tarsal glands, the forehead glands of dominant bucks are more active than those of subordinate bucks, creating much darker hair. Unlike tarsal glands, however, forehead glands contain more sudoriferous glands than sebaceous glands. These odors serve as a chemical message to other deer, indicating a buck's dominance.

The Deer I Killed Had a Wound with Pus— Can I Eat the Meat?

Pus is caused by the deer's body fighting an infection. Therefore, the meat around the wound was probably tainted. I am surprised the meat did not have a bad odor. I would not eat the meat as the infection would be carried throughout the body by the blood.

What Does the Snort-Wheeze Indicate?

Comparing the snort-wheeze to a loud cat hiss is an apt description. I have worked with captive cougars, and their raspy hissing is similar to a whitetail's snort-wheeze. Deer produce this sound, a sign of extreme aggression, by forcing air through their closed mouth and nostrils. The resulting vibrations create the hissing sound.

In a plausible scenario, a nearby buck, thinking two bucks have invaded his territory, might respond to a hunter's rattling by warning bucks in the area to stay away from "his" doe. Although a buck might broadcast the snort-wheeze without actually seeing a buck, the call is usually reserved for moments of extreme aggression.

I Killed a Doe, Then Noticed Its Accompanying Yearling Seemed Disoriented—Why?

Yearling does commonly accompany their mothers if they have no fawns, but they do not depend on their mothers for survival. The yearling would have no problem surviving winter. Most two- to two-and-a-half-month-old fawns can survive without their mother's milk. It's highly unusual for a fawn not to be weaned by four months. After that, its mother's guidance increases its survival chances, but it's not dependent on her. The yearling doe was likely with the older doe, not out of necessity, but because she wanted to be.

Fawns stay with their mother until they are almost one year old. Before giving birth to her next set of fawns, a doe drives off her yearlings and any other deer from her birthing territory. Yearlings wander, bed, and feed in the corridors and edges of these birthing territories. This exclusion from familiar home range is why so many yearlings are killed by automobiles in late May and early June.

About 50 percent of yearling bucks disperse for good at this time. Telemetry records show that most of them move up to 5 miles away. When a doe's fawns are about two weeks old, she no longer

Stamping a front foot is a sign of extreme nervousness.

Deer stoop low to produce the momentum needed to jump when frightened.

defends the birthing territory. Yearlings that did not relocate rejoin their mothers. Yearling bucks are usually driven off again just before the breeding season. These young bucks also move about 5 miles away, greatly reducing the chance of inbreeding.

Do Dogs That Chase Deer Improve the Herd Quality?

To review basics, most canines—wolves, coyotes, foxes, and dogs—kill their prey by chasing it. Foxes often kill mice by stalking, but this is an exception. Predators are more likely to kill sick or injured prey because such animals are easier to catch. Canines, however, often use teamwork to kill large, healthy prey. I've seen it happen. Dogs are descended from wolves through selective breeding. Dogs have retained the wolf's chasing instinct, which is why they run after balls, cars, and deer.

Today, about 30 million deer inhabit North America, and about 40 million domestic dogs live in the United States. It might be natural for dogs to chase deer, but it's not beneficial to deer herds. For example, in northern states, dogs are serious threats to deer.

Do Does Make an Alarm Cough?

I have heard does make coughing sounds on only a few occasions. Does usually express alarm by snorting.

Can a Yearling Have Twins?

I have not recorded yearling does giving birth to twins, but I am sure it occurs in areas such as Illinois, Wisconsin, Minnesota, Indiana, and Iowa where the soil is exceptionally deep and productive. Researchers have recorded six- to seven-month-old buck fawns that weigh 130 pounds. For a doe fawn to breed at six to seven months of age, it must weigh 70 to 80 pounds. Six- to seven-month-old doe fawns that reach 90 to 100 pounds would certainly be capable of having twins.

David Burke, from the New Jersey Fish and Game Department, said his agency has had reports of doe fawns giving birth to twins. This information was taken from roadkill records. The births happened in prime agricultural areas where fawns have excellent nutrition and are thus in prime condition when bred. He also suggests doe fawns bearing twins might have been early fawns themselves.

Are Accidental Deer Deaths Common?

Deer accidents are more frequent than reported. Because they occur in remote areas, however, they often go undiscovered. I have been living with deer for sixty-eight years, and in that time I have only seen two dozen deer killed in accidents that weren't automobile related.

One of the oddest accidents I've seen occurred when an 11 pointer rubbed his forehead on a pine tree with two 8-inch trunks. The buck became trapped when his left main beam slipped between the two trunks while rubbing. The buck's efforts to escape forced the antler tighter into the crack. Fortunately, the buck did not suffer long. The leaves around the base of the tree were kicked away, but the earth was not torn up. The buck tore the left antler beam from the skull, leaving a $1^1/2$-inch piece of jagged skull bone on the antler. This piece pierced the deer's brain, killing it. My son and I photographed the deer, then with the help of a friend tried to lift it and free the antler, which proved futile. I had to cut the broken antler from the skull to release the deer from the tree's grasp. Even then, the three of us could not pull the antler out of the cleft. There was no way the deer could have freed itself.

How Often Do Deer Defecate?

A deer probably defecates thirteen times in a twenty-four-hour period during winter, but more often during the rest of the year. A few years ago, researcher John Ozoga noted that I had taken that figure from research instead of from my own observations. Ozoga said thirteen defecations a day is probably correct during winter when a deer's metabolism is low and access to food is reduced. I have now found that deer with a good source of food in spring, summer, and fall defecate about once every forty-five minutes, or about thirty times in twenty-four hours. I assume this pattern is the same at night. I also found these figures are about the same for all herbivores because they eat a lot of bulky food.

How Does Wind Affect Deer?

The poorest time to hunt deer is during high winds. If the wind blows more than 20 MPH, deer seek heavily sheltered areas because wind robs them of their ability to detect danger by scent or sound. Healthy adult deer can stand extremely cold weather, but they won't tolerate wind in cold weather. To avoid heat loss, which expends a lot of calories, northern deer yard in the winter. In spring, summer, and early fall, deer love windstorms because they, blow down thousands of protein-rich foods like leaves and acorns.

How Does Wind Affect Deer Travel?

When a buck travels, it usually has a destination in mind, and therefore doesn't worry about wind direction. Also, when there is a lot of hunting pressure, bucks don't consider the wind when they are pushed. Their aim is only to get distance between themselves and hunters.

They can't smell properly while running. Once a buck gets into its bedding area, it usually heads into the wind, then turns and lies with its back to the wind so it can watch the trail. A buck relies on its nose to detect danger upwind and its eyes to detect danger downwind. I have seen this after following deer tracks in the snow.

The Deer I Killed Seemed Healthy but Had a Hole in Its Skull—Any Explanation?

The hole was probably made during a fight the previous year. I've seen several bucks die because their opponent's antlers penetrated their skulls. The fight probably occurred the previous year because, as you described, the punctured hole had been replaced.

The original dime-sized hole you describe is the size of an antler tine. The two small holes you describe remained open because of the draining fluid. The skull plate is thicker on the injured side because additional calcium was needed to fill in the puncture hole, thus adding thickness to that area of the skull. The added calcium and thickened plate would create a lopsided rack.

Although head wounds are not uncommon, the buck was fortunate to survive. The brain lacks extensive sensory nerves, so pain was probably minimal. If the brain is damaged, however, other body parts are inevitably affected. Because this buck, according to your account, displayed full rutting activity, its brain was probably undamaged.

This buck's eye was severely damaged in a fight with another buck during rutting season.

I Once Noticed a Deer with a Strong Odor, and There Was Phlegm in Its Bed—Any Explanation?

The deer might have been gut-shot or suffered some other type of wound to its abdomen. The phlegmlike discharge probably came from the deer's lower body cavity. The strong odor is typical of putrefaction and bacterial infection, as is the yellowish green color you described. I doubt the deer's meat could have been eaten. You probably wouldn't be able to stand the deer's putrid odor, let alone eat its venison.

Can a Dog Catch a Deer?

Large, well-fed dogs can catch adult deer, especially in winter when deer are not as well nourished. Crusty snow also helps dogs, because deer hooves break through, whereas a dog's weight is supported. Literature on the subject gives conflicting reports. The most extensive, documented studies have been done in southern states, and indicate dogs are usually unable to catch deer. Because of mild winters, lack of snow, and more food, however, southern deer are in better shape and not as vulnerable as northern deer. Because most southern waters are ice-free in winter, southern deer can escape by swimming. Northern deer cannot.

In the North, free-ranging dogs are perhaps the deer's greatest enemy aside from natural starvation. I've seen the devastation feral dogs can inflict on deer. Thankfully, pets are not allowed to run loose in most of the United States, something that should be mandatory statewide for all northern states.

When dogs—particularly small dogs—chase deer, they usually don't kill them. Running makes deer burn calories, however, which can't be easily replaced with limited food intake. This exertion also makes deer vulnerable to pneumonia-like illnesses. When deer are pursued, they usually run in a large circle so they can remain in their home range, where they know the terrain intimately. Their best chance of survival is to stay in that area. If deer are driven from their home ranges, they usually return within twenty-four hours.

Deer use a rotary gait when running—the hind feet coming down in front of the forefeet—which allows them to spring into the air to complete the cycle.

How Can I Measure a Deer Fetus?

You can use an ordinary ruler and make a rough estimate. Take the measurements from the top of the forehead, or the front of the crown, to the base of the tail. A 90-day fetus usually measures $6^{1}/_{2}$ inches. A 120-day fetus measures $10^{1}/_{2}$ inches, and a 150-day fetus measures 18 inches. From this, you can estimate the conception date.

What Are an Orphaned Fawn's Chances of Survival?

Orphaned fawns that are younger than five weeks old have practically no chance of surviving. Although research indicates some fawns are adopted, most will die if they are orphaned before they are weaned. Fawns are usually weaned by the time they're twelve weeks old.

A fawn orphaned after four months of age should most likely be able to survive on its own.

Does bond themselves to their fawn from the moment the fawn is born. In fact, a doe memorizes the smell, taste, and sounds of her fawn. After imprinting her fawn's characteristics, a doe could find the fawn among hundreds of others. Fawns are imprinted on their mother's odor, but they don't pay as much attention to it as their mother does. This can be seen by watching a large group of does and fawns feeding together in July and August. Fawns often run toward and attempt to nurse from the nearest doe, especially if the doe is nursing another fawn. The fawn wants to suckle, but the doe won't let it. The doe usually sniffs the fawn's anal gland or tarsal glands and knows instantly if the fawn is hers. The doe typically

The doe grooms her newborn fawn and eats all of the fawn's body waste when it nurses.

becomes aggressive, and she might kick the strange fawn. Captive does often nurse orphaned fawns, so I'm sure it happens occasionally in the wild. Mortality for fawns under the best of conditions runs as high as 40 percent, and fawns of does killed in June and July are part of that percentage.

Do Deer Travel along Riverbanks Only at Night?

If there's food available and no disturbances, deer should use the riverbank all year. Banks usually have plenty of sunlight, so there is an excess of grass and brush. Most floodplains, or levees, are vegetation covered and make ideal spring and summer feeding areas for deer. I wouldn't expect much deer activity at midday, but you should see deer in the morning and afternoon during spring and summer.

Are Bucks' and Does' Hoofprints Different?

It is difficult to positively distinguish the tracks of a buck from a doe. A big buck's tracks will be larger than a big doe's, but that same doe will have larger and deeper tracks than a small buck. This was a common occurrence in my area when we had a buck-only hunting season. About 86 percent of our bucks were killed when they were eighteen months old, while the big does lived to be ten to twelve years old. Naturally, the older does made larger tracks than the yearling bucks.

There are ways to tell the difference. Bucks' hooves usually have blunt tips because bucks are heavier and they travel more, especially during the rut. Most four-hooved animals step into the tracks of their front hooves with their hind hooves. When does walk, they have a slightly longer step with their hind hooves than bucks. A doe's hind hoof covers the front portion of the front-hoof track, while a buck's hind hoof only covers the back portion of the front-hoof track.

There is also a difference in stride. When walking, a mature buck has a stride of 18 to 20 inches from toe tip to toe tip. A doe's stride is about 16 inches. If there is less than $1/2$ inch of snow on the ground, deer tracks are easy to interpret. A buck's tracks in $1/2$ inch of snow will always have drag marks in front of the track. Does are daintier than bucks and pick their hoof clear of the snow. Once the snow is deeper than $1/2$ inch, all deer leave drag marks.

How Common Are Piebalds?

I am glad you used the word "piebald" instead of "albino." Most people call these mutant deer albinos, even though a true albino is pure white with pink eyes. Piebalds and albinos are genetically inferior and can be detrimental to the herd's gene pool.

Piebald deer can and do breed, and their offspring might be mutant or have normal coloration. Statistics state that piebalds occur in less than .05 percent of the population, although I believe the figure is closer to .005 percent. In most areas of the country, humans have wiped out natural predators, like wolves and cougars, that normally eliminate mutant deer. The absence of these predators, along with the addition of protective laws in some states, has allowed mutants to become more common.

Mutants are physically inferior in many respects. Most have hearing difficulties or structural problems. Their legs might be short compared with their body length, or they might have a lowered back, crooked nose, or splayed hooves.

As a result, mutant deer are frequently shunned by normally colored deer. It's not uncommon, however, for well-fed buck fawns to attempt to mount their mother or other young fawns. It also means the buck has not yet been shunned. Rejection can begin when the mother chases the mutant away to give birth to her next fawns. It will be interesting to see if other bucks associate with the mutant next spring.

What Can You Tell Me about Key Deer?

Key deer are the smallest subspecies of whitetails. By comparison, Key deer are somewhat smaller than Carmen Mountain whitetails found in the Chisos Mountains of Big Bend, Texas. Key deer are similar to the Coues deer of Arizona, but Coues deer are larger and have larger ears.

To put it into further perspective, a large North Carolina buck (*Odocoileus virginianus virginianus*) stands 38 inches at the shoulder. An average Key buck stands only 26 to 28 inches high. In addition, an adult Key buck weighs about 80 pounds on the hoof. The average Coues buck stands 31 inches high at the shoulder and weighs 98 pounds.

Key deer are found only in the Florida Keys, and the best place to find them is the National Key Deer Refuge on Big Pine, Little Pine, Sugarloaf, and No-Name Keys. These deer are an endangered species, with an estimated population of 300. In 1950, only 50 Key deer existed. Under the Endangered Species Act, the population peaked at 400 several years ago. Unfortunately, the population is dwindling because of land development and increased automobile traffic. In fact, despite a strict 35 MPH speed limit, car-deer accidents have accounted for as many as 65 Key deer deaths annually, equal to the annual fawn crop.

Key deer are not on the same annual cycle as most other North American deer. They are a tropical subspecies, and fawns have been born in every month of the year. I have visited the region twice—both times in February—and have seen bucks with polished antlers and velvet antlers. Although the breeding cycle can last all year, I would estimate the peak of the breeding activity takes place in January and February.

Are Turkey and Deer Populations Competitors?

According to research reports from Vermont, Pennsylvania, and Virginia, turkeys do not seriously compete with deer for food because their diets are not similar enough to make a difference. In my opinion, however, turkeys in some instances can pose huge competition for acorns. I have photographed wild turkeys and deer feeding side by side with neither paying attention to the other. These instances took place in grass fields, however, not noisy autumn woodlots.

It's possible that deer would avoid turkeys in a dry autumn woods. Under such conditions, deer can't possibly hear danger coming because of the noise made by the turkeys. That makes them nervous. On a side note, I have seen deer turn violent when competing with turkeys for acorns. Deer will use their hooves to strike turkeys when they come too close. Conversely, I have seen turkeys flap their wings and jump at fawns.

Turkeys are not the only birds that annoy whitetails. I once watched a Canada goose drive deer away from a pond where other geese were nesting. When deer approached the pond to drink, the gander would fly directly at their heads. Like the turkeys mentioned earlier, the goose went after the smaller deer.

Why Would Deer Frequent Human-Scented Spots?

Deer would not frequent a human-scented spot if the area was open to hunting because hunted whitetails typically alter their habits after encountering humans. It wouldn't be unusual for the deer to tolerate human presence, however, if the area was closed to hunting. Unpressured whitetails become habituated to seeing people, and will go about their daily routine. Still, these deer will show caution when humans try to get too close to them.

I Once Saw a Small Doe with a Fawn Chase a Bigger Doe— Is This Normal?

When it comes to whitetails, nothing can be termed "normal." It is true, however, that in most cases larger deer will chase smaller deer from food sources. In the wild, size and strength determine dominance. The exception in your case was the small doe had a fawn with her, while the big one did not.

The ferocity and devotion of the maternal instinct is well-known. Before giving birth, does have a birthing territory, and they drive all other deer from it. After giving birth, they defend this territory fiercely for about two weeks. The fawn you saw was probably one to two weeks old. At that age, the doe would have given up the birthing territory, but she might have established a protective zone around her fawn. This protectiveness diminishes as fawns grow older. By winter, the larger doe (that was run off) would surely run the younger does away from food sources.

Does a Deer's Color Change from Year to Year?

A deer's hide color is the same, during the same season, from year to year. Because of genetics, deer hair widely varies in color even in deer from the same region. Deer that live in more open country tend to have lighter-colored coats than deer that live in dark conifer forests and dense cedar swamps. In warm-blooded animals, dark pigments are most prevalent in warm, humid habitats. The winter coat of all deer becomes lighter just before it is shed in May. Deer can have light-colored coats, however, if they are exposed to excessive sunlight.

Do You Think a Broadhead-Grazed Buck Will Return Next Year?

It's unlikely the buck has left the area since it's his home range. Deer move when they disperse as youngsters, but once they have settled in an area, they seldom leave, and can't really be pushed out. They are safest in their home range, because they know the area intimately. Chances are, however, your buck is now much more cautious.

I Don't See Scrapes on My Hunting Grounds Anymore— How Come?

If you are not seeing as many deer, it's possible that you have over-hunted the land. You might have put too much pressure on the deer herd and, therefore, severely reduced its size. A more likely scenario, however, is the farmland has matured and no longer provides quality deer habitat. Without adequate browse, hunting land can "dry up" in a hurry. In addition, food crops in the area might have changed so the area is no longer attractive to deer.

Why Would a Deer Charge a Person?

Each year some hunters are attacked and even occasionally killed by white-tailed bucks. In the two instances you mention, I believe it was a case of mistaken identity. When the buck started his charge, he thought he was charging another deer. This could have happened if you were using deer lure, especially buck urine. Even stepping behind a tree would not deter a buck from attacking if you were his intended target. In both cases, the buck probably discovered his mistake while charging.

My Buck Had Really Long Eyelashes—What's Normal?

Unlike humans, deer have eyelashes on just the upper eyelid. A deer eyelid has about forty-six hairs, so your buck was average in that respect. Above the eyelid are about eighteen hairs that are about 3 inches long, with some 4 inches long. There are about eighteen hairs scattered below the eye that are 3 inches or longer. The rest of the lashes measure in the 1-inch range. All of these hairs act as sensory devices, like a cat's whiskers, to warn deer of brush or other vegetation that could harm the eye.

CHAPTER 4

Hunting Advice

Where Should I Aim?

If the deer is standing still at close range and you are confident with your shooting, aim for the middle of the neck. A shot in the neck usually severs the vertebrae, dropping the deer in its tracks. This will also cause the least amount of meat loss. Do not shoot a buck in the neck if you plan to have the head mounted.

If the neck does not provide a certain shot, aim 4 to 6 inches from the bottom of the deer's rib cage, and about 4 inches from the foreleg elbow. The shot should penetrate the heart and kill the deer almost instantly. With the exception of gut shots, I recommend following a wounded deer immediately to keep it bleeding. A deer has to lose about three pints of blood before dying. The more active the deer, the quicker it loses blood and the sooner it will die. A wounded deer that is allowed to bed down might stop bleeding. Hunters should wait at least an hour before trailing gut-shot deer.

How Should I Store Unused Buck Lure?

Scent and urine should be packaged in dark-colored glass. I've had no problem using scent from one year to the next by keeping it tightly sealed and stored in a dark area. Open the bottles briefly the

Unless you are an excellent marksman, do not shoot a running deer—you might merely wound it.

night before using them so you can let the ammonia escape. You can prevent scent from evaporating by tightly resealing the bottle caps.

Are Cover and Attractant Scents Really Necessary?

I believe that anyone who bowhunts without using scent is not going to be as successful as someone who does. Scents are not as important to gun hunters, particularly where there is heavy hunting pressure. A cover scent is not important if you always stay downwind of deer. Wind often swirls, however, and wind direction changes; so I recommend using cover scents.

Washing your clothing in baking soda is a good scent nullifier. Keep your hunting clothes in a clean plastic bag, hung outside where they won't get wet or contaminated. You might want to put some evergreen sprigs in the bag. A pair of rubbers slipped on over your hunting shoes after you get away from the car will reduce your scent trail, but so long as you are a living, breathing human being, you are going to produce scent that cannot be eliminated. What you eat, your body chemistry, and how much you perspire contribute to the scent you produce. Avoid eating onions, garlic, peppers, and other foods that produce bad breath and ooze out your pores. Wash with unscented soap such as Ivory.

I do not recommend skunk scent as a cover scent. I believe that wild creatures know skunks discharge scent only when frightened. I use fox urine as a cover scent because foxes are not a threat to deer, and deer encounter fox scent routinely. Deer urine is also an excellent cover scent. Being 15 feet off the ground will prevent deer from getting your scent, but only if it is warm and thermals are rising. It will not prevent deer from scenting you on a cool morning when your scent falls to the ground.

Bucks are able to smell danger a greater distance on a foggy day because the scent molecules stay close to the earth.

Tarsal glands are one of the best cover and attractant scents, but they have a usage time limit. After cutting off a 4-inch piece of skin, including the gland, hang the gland to dry and it's ready to use. Keep it in an airtight bag when not in use. Remember, after the gland's removal from a deer, no more scent is being produced; and with each usage, more scent evaporates. By storing the glands properly, they should last a season. Glands that you take from your deer in the gun season can be put in a plastic bag and frozen till next season.

A new scent might cause deer to shy away. By the same token, deer are very curious, and a new scent may pique a deer's interest. A curious deer is an alert deer, however; and any sound or movement will send it dashing away. In the pre-rut, food scents work best. Use white oak acorn scent if you can get it. Apple scent is also good. From mid-October on, use a sex scent. In addition to doe-in-heat scent, buck urine also works well.

What's the Best Way to Rattle Post-Rut?

Rattling does not work nearly as well in the post-rut as it does in the pre-rut. Rattling works best just before a doe's estrous period. For most of the country north of the 32nd parallel, that would be the last week in October and the first week in November. I don't know your reason for hunting after the rut, but I suggest you change your hunt to the pre-rut, if possible.

In the post-rut, bucks are exhausted, almost all of the breeding is done, and bucks are concentrating on feeding. When you start to rattle, tick your antlers together lightly. The sound will carry a long distance on calm days. Banging the antlers loudly at the beginning might scare off nearby bucks. Tick the antlers together half a dozen times and wait five minutes. If nothing shows, bang them together lightly. Wait another five minutes. If nothing appears, bang the antlers together loudly, each time banging and twisting them a half dozen times or more.

For the fourth series, crash them together and wait ten minutes. I have found that small bucks have a tendency to tiptoe into the area. They don't want to be caught off guard by a big buck. Big bucks tend to charge in because they are looking for a fight. Blow a grunt call as you bang the antlers together. Set the O-ring at the

A buck can often be brought in by the sound of antlers being rattled.

lowest pitch. All of the bucks I've heard give an exceptionally low blat of about two to three seconds in duration.

How Can I Keep My Glasses from Fogging?

Thankfully, I don't need glasses while I am hunting, although I do need them for reading. I encounter fogging when I am looking through the viewfinder of my camera in cold weather. I have tried different antifogging gels on my viewfinder without any real success. I've been told that Barbasol shaving cream works well, and I intend to field-test it when the weather cools down. You might want to give that a try.

Does Human Urine Spook Deer?

I think it depends. Except in wilderness areas, most deer probably encounter so much human scent that it probably doesn't trigger as much of an alarm as it used to. I think fresh human scent still alerts every deer, but traces of human scent may not. Before I became a photographer and deer researcher, I was a fox trapper. To successfully trap foxes, I had to eliminate as much human scent as possible. To be a successful deer hunter, I believe that you have to eliminate as much human scent as possible as well.

I would never urinate anywhere near my tree stand. Some hunters claim that they urinate in the scrapes they hunt over. I wouldn't do that. Some hunters claim that deer will come to regular household ammonia because they are attracted to the ammonia in urine. When not hunting, I have run a number of tests using household ammonia without ever attracting a deer.

When Are Deer Most Likely to Visit a Water Source?

Factors such as body size and time of year determine how much water deer need. Under controlled conditions, a large buck eating dry feed and hay will drink about 8 quarts of water per day. In the wild, whitetails are seldom farther than 2 miles from water.

Snow and ice are available in winter in the North, so deer don't need to visit a water source. In spring, new vegetation, which has a high water content, supplies daily water intake, as do raindrops and dew. During these months, deer will probably drink water only if they pass it. Most vegetation dries in summer, so deer will go to water at least once a day. In July and August, deer browse near ponds and lakes, feeding on water plants and filamentous algae, and escaping from heat and biting insects. At this time, deer frequent water sources in late afternoon and early morning. In farming areas, deer visit ponds by choice; but in wilderness areas, they often must feed at ponds because little vegetation is growing in the forest. In autumn, most crops have dried, but deer still get moisture from newly fallen leaves.

If drought conditions occur, deer must go to water at least twice a day. Deer might visit watering areas in the dark, so I would check the edges of ponds and rivers. Deer drink in the same area each day, so you should set up your stand where tracks are concentrated.

Does Flash Photography Affect Deer?

Flash, without other noise, does not adversely affect wild animals. They are too accustomed to lightning. In the 1890s, when George Shiras III used flash powder to take his famous deer photos at night, it was the explosion that scared deer, not the light. He nevertheless obtained fantastic photos.

I do not believe using cameras in one location would drive deer from that area. Deer can become accustomed to almost any disturbance that does not harm them. Note deer feeding along highways, despite the roar of traffic and bright lights. Deer often feed on army artillery ranges, even when shells are exploding.

How Should I Best Use a Remote Camera?

Scouting will reveal the main travel routes. The best place to put your camera is between feeding and bedding areas. Where legal, bait the deer, although make sure no bait shows in your photographs. Set your camera to take the photo as deer come to the bait.

I would definitely want a camera unit to be tripped by a photoelectric cell or infrared beam, rather than a string. A string can be broken, and I don't understand how you could take multiple photos with a string. I would want a camera that had a motor wind and an electronic flash so the unit could work on everything that passed by. By raising the triggering beam to 24 inches above the ground, the camera could record every deer, but would not be tripped by smaller animals, such as skunks, opossums, or raccoons. If you want to photograph them, set the beam to 10 inches off the ground.

Are Decoys Worth the Effort?

Use decoys whenever possible, but only during bow season—it is too dangerous during gun season. If you carry a full-sized decoy, wrap it in blaze orange so it is not mistaken for a real deer. Decoys do several things. Most important, they direct a deer's attention away from you. Second, they pacify deer, because incoming deer know another deer would not be in the area if a human was also there. During the rut, a decoy might induce incoming deer to throw caution to the wind. If you use a grunt call or rattle antlers, the deer that respond will expect to see another deer.

I often use a decoy when photographing; and I agree that it's difficult, and perhaps dangerous, to carry a full-bodied decoy into the woods. I have instead been using two Renzo's silhouette decoys. These are foldable, waterproof, life-sized silhouettes that come complete with the rods to keep them upright. The two decoys together weigh just $1^1/_2$ pounds. I use a buck and doe and place them at right angles to each other so that no matter where a deer stands, it will see one of the silhouettes full form.

Do Deer Cover Disturbed Scrapes?

No, I don't believe bucks cover their scrapes. I believe the covered scrape you describe was found by another hunter who kicked leaves in it to see if the scrape was being used. I often do this myself to find out the last time the scrape was used. Kicking leaves in a scrape will not prevent a buck from using it, and it will tell you when the scrape was last used.

Can Deer Hear Sounds We Can't?

Yes, deer can hear far beyond our capability. Do not wear a hard-surfaced jacket in the woods. That's why many top deer hunters swear by wool, cotton, and/or fleece jackets. These garments, along with many high-tech fabrics, nearly eliminate noise from twigs and such. A deer's large, funnel-shaped ears can pick up far more sound waves than we can, and they also hear lots of sounds that are beyond the hearing range of the human ear. I've proven this countless times by blowing a silent dog whistle to get a deer's attention when photographing. Dogs and deer can hear the sound, but humans cannot.

Hunting clothing should have a soft or napped finish. Many deer are spooked when they hear the arrow being drawn. No sound that we can hear is too slight to escape detection by a deer.

My Arrow Indicated That I Gut-Shot a Buck.
I Saw the Deer Seemingly Healthy Sometime Later but Could Never Recover It, Which Bothers Me Greatly— Could It Have Survived?

I fully realize your agonizing over wounding an animal and then not recovering it. I once had the same thing happen to me. Gut-shot deer sometimes live because the arrow did not hit enough vitals,

Bucks paw scrapes to get down to the bare earth.

veins, or arteries to cause substantial blood loss. Such instances, however, are rare.

A brown film on an arrow is definitely from stomach contents. The fact that you saw the same buck sixteen days later in apparently good health gives evidence that he survived to see another hunting season. A big buck's chances of survival are better than those of a smaller deer. The saying, "the bigger they are, the harder they fall" definitely rings true in deer hunting.

Some folks might get upset to hear that you wounded a deer you did not recover. Be concerned, but don't despair. It's sometimes unavoidable. You should be commended for doing everything in your power to try to recover the deer and for renewing your commitment to doing everything you can to prevent it from happening again.

I Want to Bowhunt from the Ground—Any Advice?

First, I must assume you're proficient with your bow. Before even thinking about heading to the woods, you must be able to consistently put all of your arrows into a 6-inch circle at 20 yards. Although many bowhunting shots are less than that distance, it is a good starting point.

After setting a standard, such as 20 yards, never shoot at deer that are farther away. The last thing you want to do is wound a deer and lose it. Also, never shoot at a deer that is facing you. Take a bowhunter education course and learn about the various shot angles.

Although the quartering-away shot is best for bowhunting, the broadside shot is also acceptable. When shooting at a deer, visualize the same 6-inch circle you use for practice. On a deer, that circle would be just behind the front leg and about 4 inches up from the bottom of the rib cage. That will put your arrow through both lungs or through the lungs and the heart. Don't shoot at a running deer or even one that's trotting. Stop the deer by blowing softly on a grunt call or by making a bleating sound with your voice.

Although many bowhunters prefer ground blinds, I recommend that you learn how to hunt from a tree stand. Tree stands provide hunters with the element of surprise, allowing for closer

A hunter may be able to get this trotting buck, to stop in a perfect position for a shot, by blowing a grunt call.

shots. If you insist on using a ground blind, build one out of brush or camouflage material so deer won't see you move when they step within shooting range.

Although camouflage clothing isn't an absolute necessity, it greatly improves your odds of getting close to whitetails. It's especially important to cover up the shine from your face and hands. Use gloves and a face mask and invest in some inexpensive camouflage makeup. Wind direction is more important than what you wear. Your blind or tree stand has to be downwind of the deer, and this is far more important if you hunt from the ground. Another advantage to hunting from a tree stand is that under favorable conditions, scent often disperses before it reaches the ground.

If you are new to bowhunting, I suggest you forget about big bucks and focus on simply getting close to deer. Period. This is going to involve a lot of scouting. Walk your hunting grounds in spring and summer and learn the feeding and bedding areas. Locate major deer trails and learn how deer use them to enter and exit their bedding areas. Pay attention to wind direction and choose stand sites accordingly. You will probably learn that some trails are only used at night. This will help you formulate better hunting plans. Learn the best time to use calls and lures. Grunt calls, doe-in-heat lure, and rattling antlers are good tactics to use when hunting this period.

How Can I Avoid Lyme Disease?

Lyme disease spreads rapidly and has many hosts besides deer. Deer get the bulk of the blame, although mice are probably a greater problem simply because of their numbers. More than forty species of birds also carry the deer tick. The mild winter of 1997–98 increased the tick population, but the greatest boon to tick survival has probably been the prohibition of burning high, dead-grass fields, which are perfect habitat for ticks. When farmers were forced to stop burning grass and stubble fields, tick populations soared.

In my close association with deer, I have been fortunate to avoid Lyme disease. In fact, it's been years since I've even found a tick on me. I constantly saturate my pants, socks, and shoes with Repel Permanone, a chemical killer/repellent developed by the U.S. Air Force. Although it isn't harmful, Repel Permanone isn't intended for use on skin. It can be bought at *www.rue.com* or in sporting goods stores. Most doctors now recognize the symptoms of Lyme disease, which they couldn't do a few years ago. Most bite sites are identifiable by a red bull's-eye accompanied by chills and fever. If you suspect Lyme disease, get to a doctor fast. When properly diagnosed, the disease can be easily treated with antibiotics.

Can Ticks Spread Something other than Lyme Disease?

I believe the disease to which you are referring is human ehrlichiosis. I haven't heard much about it lately, but I read a scientific paper on it several years ago. The lone star tick, which is common in the

South, is the transmitter of the rickettsial organism known as *Ehrlichia chaffeensis*. Deer, raccoons, foxes, and rabbits are known to have the ticks and the *Ehrlichia* organisms. To date, about 400 cases have been identified. The symptoms are fever, headaches, chills, aching muscles, sweating, nausea, and vomiting. The patient can be cured with antibiotics.

Take great care when in high-grass areas in summer and early fall. Saturate your clothing with Repel Permanone, which kills ticks on contact. You don't have to wear a surgical scrub outfit; you do have to take precautions. If the deer you shoot has ticks, have someone check you for ticks after you gut your deer. If you hang your deer overnight, ticks should leave it as soon as the body heat has left the carcass.

How Far Can Deer Hear Rattling and Grunt Calls?

There are no hard-and-fast answers to this question. Too many variables enter the picture to make more than an educated guess. Humidity, temperature, wind direction, and ambient sounds affect a deer's ability to hear and smell. Their ability to detect calling also depends on how often you grunt and rattle.

Generally, deer can hear rattling from more than a quarter mile. For example, while hunting in Texas, my guide rattled in a buck from about that distance. Because of the buck's immediate and aggressive behavior, I theorize it could have heard the rattling from a longer distance. On the other hand, deer most likely can't hear grunting at more than 300 yards because of its low tone. If you're being detected a lot it's probably because you're grunting too often. Calling directs attention to your location. If you call too much, deer will pinpoint you before you see them. To prevent this, allow at least ten minutes to pass between calling sessions. This is especially important while rattling, which requires added movement. Also consider that although some bucks respond aggressively to calling, most approach cautiously, looking for the sound's source. When the temperature is between 60 and 70 degrees, the humidity is 50 percent to 70 percent, and the wind is 2 to 3 MPH, deer can probably smell estrous doe urine from at least 1 mile. A deer's sense of smell is thousands of times better than that of humans.

Will Washing Eliminate or Add Odors to My Camouflage?

Use UV-eliminating, scent-free detergents. Years ago, most camouflage was made with UV brighteners, which deer can see. Most modern camouflage is not, but conventional UV detergents add brighteners, making camouflage more visible to deer.

How Should I Age My Venison?

Venison should be cooled at 34 to 38 degrees for at least ten days to be properly aged. You can age venison in a refrigerator if you have the space and can maintain the proper temperature. This is difficult, however, because frequent opening and closing makes it nearly impossible to keep the temperature constant. Having a butcher age your venison might be possible. Some states, however, prohibit hanging deer in the same cooler with regularly processed meats.

In the absence of a walk-in cooler, most hunters are best served to field-dress their deer within ten minutes of killing it. Prompt removal of internal organs and blood is crucial for good-tasting venison. Then, hang the deer by its head. I believe this helps the carcass drain better. Finally, prop the rib cage open with an 8-inch stick to quickly cool the inside of the carcass. Let the deer hang overnight, and then butcher it the next morning. Even if the temperature drops below freezing overnight, the meat usually does not freeze. These methods ensure good-tasting venison without the hassle of aging.

Can Rattling Attract Bears?

Yes. Bears kill whitetails, particularly fawns. A bear attracted to rattling might have never found deer locked together, but it probably knew fighting deer are not alert to danger because they are concentrating on their opponent. Predators are opportunists and are sensitive to the slightest deviation from normal behavior. Any indication of a prey's handicap can trigger an attack from a predator.

Can Rattling Attract Horses?

A horse would have no interest in a fight between bucks, but it might be curious about the unfamiliar sound.

How Can I Rig My Shotgun for Muzzleloading?

Shotgun receivers are built to withstand ordinary explosive pressure produced by smokeless shotgun shells. They are not designed for igniting loose powder and shooting patched balls. The bottom line is this: *Never, under any circumstances, alter a firearm!* Besides the obvious danger involved, I can't imagine why anyone would want to do such a thing. Aside from being illegal for use during a muzzleloader season (shotguns don't qualify as primitive weapons), shotguns rigged this way would provide no performance advantage over conventional muzzleloaders.

Although it didn't involve muzzleloading equipment, I encountered similar tampering with guns while working as a deputy game warden for New Jersey. I arrested a man and confiscated his gun for tampering with his buckshot shells. At the time, only buckshot was legal for deer hunting in New Jersey. To get around this, the hunter removed the wad from the end of the shell and poured melted lead around the shot to make a sort of slug. I spoiled his day by arresting him, but I might have saved his hand and perhaps his life. If fired, the solid chunk of lead would have probably plugged his barrel and made it explode.

Will Field-Dressing Contaminate a Hunting Area?

Maybe. To be safe, move your deer at least 100 yards before field-dressing it if you plan to reuse your stand. I have never seen a deer actually leave an area because of a gut pile. Deer are often more curious than frightened by it. I don't want gut piles near my stand, however, because they make deer exceedingly cautious.

Will a Stand Affect Short Crossbow Shots?

You do not have to adjust your aim to compensate for stand height. The idea of aiming low from a tree stand is a fallacy. There's no difference in the pull of gravity. Aiming low might counteract a deer's tendency to squat at the sound of the shot, but arrow speed should compensate for that, especially at just 15 yards. If you can consistently hit your target while shooting from the ground, you should do just as well from a 10- to 12-foot-tall tree stand.

I Hunt Alone—If I Kill a Deer, How Can I Field-Dress It?

Field-dress a deer immediately after killing it, using a knife with a 3-inch blade. Cut a circle around the deer's anus, and use the blade to loosen the tube from the walls of the pelvic arch. Roll the deer on its back and straddle its rib cage, facing the hind legs. I position the deer's front legs outside my legs to help hold the deer upright.

Grasp the skin of the belly, pull upward, and insert the blade a half-inch under the skin. If the deer has just died, the paunch and entrails will fall away from the skin. If the deer is starting to bloat when you find it, cut carefully, because the gas in the paunch and intestines will cause these organs to push out through the hole.

After inserting the blade, cut through the skin and tissue in a straight line, through the underbelly and around the penis or udder. Then, if the deer is a buck, cut through the penis. Then, turn around and cut through the ribs off to the side of the breastbone. Do not do this, however, if you intend to have a chest mount done.

Reach into the body cavity and sever the windpipe and esophagus at the base of the neck. Cut the diaphragm loose on both sides of the body cavity down to the backbone. Next, lay the deer on its side and pull out the windpipe, esophagus, lungs, heart, liver, and diaphragm wall. Cut the kidney loose from the backbone and pull out the paunch, intestines, and bladder. Place the heart and liver in a plastic bag if you plan to eat them. Remove the anus and tube through the pelvic arch, and roll everything onto the ground. Roll the deer onto its stomach with the legs spread to drain the blood. Hang the deer by its head with its hind feet about a foot above the ground to help drain the blood.

Propping the body cavity open with a stick helps the body cool faster and decreases the chance of spoilage. If you accidentally cut into the paunch or intestines, rinse the carcass with water. If the weather is cool, allow the deer to hang overnight, then butcher it the next day. If flies are present, put a mesh bag over the carcass to prevent insects laying eggs on the meat.

How Can I Find Good Hunting Land to Lease?

Contact the state conservation department to see if they have records on where the state's biggest bucks have been killed. If they do not, contact the Pope and Young Club or the Boone and Crockett Club and get their record books. I have never leased land, but my friends leased a 170-acre farm in Hunterdon County, New Jersey, for $4,000 per year. The farm is in some of the nation's best deer country; and as a result, it commands the high price.

Another friend of mine leased a Texas ranch for $65,000 a year. He killed ten bucks a year, and each had to have 10 points or more. That harvest equated to paying $6,500 per buck. These situations, however, might represent the extremes of lease prices, and probably differ from your area. Therefore, when you find where you want to hunt, contact your state's wildlife division and ask for the going rate of land leases in your area.

Should I Buy the Older Scents and Lures I See on Sale?

Many deer lures are bottled in green or amber glass to protect them from the sun's rays and to prevent oxidation. If these scents are kept sealed and stored in a cool, dark place, they should keep indefinitely. For example, when I was younger, I trapped frequently and depended on effective scents. If I stored scents properly, even bottles that had been opened then resealed worked well in subsequent years. Therefore, stock up on lures during a sale.

How Should I Transport My Deer?

First, check with game laws in your state and the state you are hunting in to see if you can transport processed venison in coolers. I know some states prohibit this. In Wisconsin, you cannot cut up a deer until it's checked at a state registration station.

Next, consider the weather. If it is cold, you can safely bring the deer home in a bag. When temperatures are warm, it is better to cut it up and pack it in ice inside a cooler. I believe in common sense, not political correctness. I do suggest, however, that hunters cover their deer while transporting them.

If you can't properly age your meat—and 99 percent of us can't—then butcher the deer as soon as the body heat has dissipated and the meat has firmed up. I always bone my venison, so there is only a fraction of the deer to bring home. If you can legally bring your deer home cut up, why not do the job at your deer camp? You have to do it anyway, and this allows you to transport a much smaller parcel home. On average, I reduce a 125-pound live-weight deer to 48 pounds of meat.

Six Nice Bucks Have Been Taken on My Small Parcel in the Past Few Years—Is the Spot Now Hunted Out?

As long as hunting pressure does not increase on neighboring prop-erties and food supplies remain the same, you should continue to experience good hunting on your property. Increased hunting pres-sure and food shortages change an area's hunting stability. Food shortages often result when woodlands mature from brushy areas to beanpole stands that choke out the understory. And because of the gradual transition, most hunters don't realize the food source has changed. If the area you hunt is adjacent to farmland and deer feed there, it should continue to produce large, healthy deer—as long as farming continues.

Which Is Better, a High-Shoulder Shot or Behind the Shoulder?

Knowledge of a deer's anatomy is a must for every hunter, because it helps cut down the incidence of wounded deer. Even some expe-rienced hunters do not know the exact location of a deer's vital organs. Hitting the shoulder blade usually knocks a deer down, and it will definitely cripple it. If the shot is in the center of the shoulder, it will also sever the spine. A deer hit there will drop instantly, making it an effective spot for a shot. The high-shoulder shot, however, will not touch the deer's heart; and it might miss the lungs, too.

To hit the heart, aim slightly behind the deer's elbow and 6 inches above the base of the rib cage. A shot there will take out the heart and lungs. A standing deer will drop quickly; and a running deer, with adrenaline coursing through its system, might run 100 yards. I recommend the book *Advanced Whitetail Details* from Krause Publications, which illustrates shot placement with a set of five acetate overlays of deer anatomy done by Wayne Trimm. We owe it to the animals we hunt to make a kill as cleanly as possible.

A running deer shot through the heart may still run 100 yards or more because of the adrenaline coursing through his body.

Can You Explain Gun Calibers and Ranges?

The designation of calibers for rifles and handguns is simple. The decimal point means a .22 bullet is $^{22}/_{100}$ of an inch in diameter. Some cartridges are designated as .243, .270, .280, or .375, meaning the diameter of the bullet is figured in thousandths of an inch. Naturally, the larger the number, the larger the bullet. Confusion comes into play with cartridges like the .30-06. The bullet is $^{30}/_{100}$ of an inch in diameter, and it was developed in 1906. Even more confusing is the .30-30, which is $^{30}/_{100}$ of an inch in diameter and was originally propelled by 30 grains of black powder.

With rifles and handguns, the larger the number, the larger the bore diameter of the barrel and bullet. Not so with shotgun gauges. With the exception of the .410, which actually has a bore of $^{410}/_{1000}$ of an inch, shotgun gauges do not designate bore size. Instead, the

10-, 12-, 16-, 20-, and 28-gauge designations indicate how many lead balls with a diameter equal to the size of the barrel are in 1 pound. A 10-gauge shotgun has ten lead balls to the pound while the 28-gauge has twenty-eight lead balls. So, unlike rifle and handgun classifications, the smaller the gauge number, the larger the bore.

How Should I Use My Rubber Boots?

When I did a lot of bowhunting, I carried my camouflage clothing and rubber boots in a plastic bag with some red cedar branches. When I got to my hunting area, I would put on my camouflage and boots. Whenever possible, I walked in manure to mask any odors. All rubber boots will work well if used in this manner.

Should I Hunt in the Rain?

Except for the rut and hunting pressure, no other factor influences deer activity as much as weather. While growing up on a farm, I noticed that if our cows went under the trees, there would be a hard but brief rain. If the cows stayed in the open and continued to feed, the storm would be gentle and prolonged.

Deer follow the same pattern. Some of the best hunting might be in a gentle, prolonged rain because deer will move and feed more than during dark, rainy nights. Though deer are active before and after a strong storm, they hold to cover through its duration. Wind also affects deer behavior. While photographing bucks during a period of unseasonably warm weather, I noticed deer would leave cover and enter fields to feed about an hour earlier on breezy days—even if the temperature was higher.

I Plan to Hunt in South Carolina in August—Any Advice?

Offering such an early season is absurd. Downed deer will probably be bloated beyond use if not found within an hour. Even if you quickly recover a deer, flies can still lay eggs on the carcass. Plus, a hunter's body odor is more likely to contaminate the area because of hot, humid weather.

You will be hunting during difficult conditions. Deer are not likely to move until after dusk and will bed before daylight. I would not use a doe-in-heat scent. Try buck urine because bucks are always interested in other bucks. Your best bet is to intercept a buck on its way to feed.

By mid-August, velvet is dry and resembles shrink-wrap. Antler damage, however, is still possible because of residual blood in the velvet. Contact your taxidermist to see what he recommends if you plan to keep the velvet on the antlers.

Where Can I Get Good Information to Defend Deer Hunting at Community Meetings?

The greatest problem in this debate is that the two sides don't speak the same language. We also, however, must recognize the rights and needs of the suburban population in this problem. While most of these folks are not antihunters, they might be against hunting as the main means of game management. It is important that hunters understand the difference, and it is important the suburban population is heard and respected. Coalitions must be formed with all sides of the issue represented. All options should be studied, and the majority of citizens should be satisfied with the final decision.

I understand what you are trying to do and commend you. I have spent a lifetime trying to do the same in my lectures and writing. The best source of up-to-date information is the booklet "An Evaluation of Deer Management Options." It can be ordered from the New Hampshire Fish and Game Department, Wildlife Division, 2 Hazen Drive, Concord, NH 03301. Send $1 for shipping. Also, the "Guide to Urban Bowhunting" is available from the National Bowhunter Education Foundation at 267 E. 29th St., Box 250, Loveland, CO 80538. These booklets present the hunter's side of the issue based upon scientific facts.

Any Advice on Stand Hunting from a Ridge?

Because you are on a ridge above them, your scent might warn deer of your presence. This could be the case for deer that move at 8 A.M., but it will not affect deer that come up at 10 A.M. By 10 A.M., the earth should warm enough for thermals to move up the ridge. Move your stand to a position that will put the wind in your favor. Set your stand 30 to 40 feet from the trail with the wind in your face; and you should be close enough for a shot.

My Favorite Cornfield is Changing to Hay—Is This the End of My Hunting Haven?

A change in crops affects the whitetail's use of an area. Many farmers raise horse hays like timothy and orchard grass instead of trefoils, alfalfa, or clover. Deer don't eat horse hays, so these areas can't support them. Restriction on food sources like this results in fewer, as well as smaller, deer. If your hunting area is planted with horse hays and grasses, the chance of getting big deer is greatly reduced. As a general rule; if you hunt for bucks where you see does feeding, you will be successful.

New Jersey Fish and Game Says One Hunter Could Legally Take 119 Deer a Year Using All Available Permits— Why Is the State Trying to Wipe out the Herd?

New Jersey had a "bucks-only" season until 1959 to build up the state's deer herd, which had dropped to less than 200 by the late 1800s. By the time New Jersey had its first doe season, deer were destroying land and crops, and deer/car accidents were increasing dramatically. Since then, the New Jersey Division of Fish and Game has done an outstanding job of managing the deer herd.

The state was divided into game-management areas that can be individually controlled. The game department is not trying to wipe out the deer herd. If anything, the department is only guilty of not educating hunters and nonhunters about the deer population.

For years, the concern of game managers in New Jersey, and across the United States, was the carrying capacity of the land, or how many deer could feed in a square mile without causing habitat destruction. They concluded that about twenty deer per square mile was the land's maximum. On less-fertile land, that number was even less.

Today, the department must also consider the social carrying capacity of the land. In other words, how much deer damage will the public tolerate? Many areas of the state have thirty or more deer per square mile. Reforestation is virtually impossible because deer eat new seedlings as fast as they sprout. The state averages between 7,000 and 8,000 deer/car collisions a year, and insurance companies figure the cost for automobile repairs averages $2,000 per accident or $14 million to $16 million annually. That's not counting the cost of medical bills.

The number quoted by the New Jersey game manager is merely an example of how high the deer population is. It is possible, although extreme, to take that many deer. This is not being done, however, on a normal basis. Game managers realize they are not just beholden to hunters, but also to landowners and the general public. Their goal is to reduce the size of the deer herd to reduce damage. The cheapest, most economical way for that to happen is to liberalize hunting seasons and game bags.

I hear this same complaint from hunters across the country. "Why is the game commission killing off all the deer?" This question has two answers, and they might seem contradictory. First, game commissions aren't conspiring to "kill all the deer." They're simply managing bulging deer herds. Second, without deer, many commission employees wouldn't have jobs. Your frustration is understandable. Deer herds we tried so hard to protect just forty years ago are now too large. Some herds, however, were too large even forty years ago. Thankfully, we passed laws that ended bucks-only hunting.

Today's deer management process is complex, especially with the fact suburbia is spreading across the country; and land that was once deer habitat is now inhabited by humans. As hunters, we would love to see more deer. We have to realize, however, that North America's whitetail population—about 30 million deer—is at an all-time high. For perspective, in 1900, there were about 100,000 whitetails in the United States. Liberal hunting seasons and bag limits are the most economical way to manage today's herds.

When herds were small, managers were mainly concerned with the land's carrying capacity. Most of today's deer herds far exceed the land's capacity, and, in most cases, to their own detriment. There's more to deer management, however, than considering the land's carrying capacity. We also have to be concerned with the land's social carrying capacity. We have to be concerned with the wishes and desires of the people who own the land, such as farmers. Many people don't want large deer herds. They might enjoy seeing a few deer, but they don't want deer destroying their crops, gardens, and shrubs, and they don't want to live with the constant fear of hitting deer with their vehicles.

If state game commissions don't take the initiative and reduce deer herds on their own terms, they will have the terms dictated to them by the voters, and there are more nonhunting voters than hunters. Unfortunately, the game department cannot satisfy everyone. Enjoy the fantastic deer hunting we have today because it is as good as it ever will be.

Any Advice on Hunting Mountainous Regions?

I have lived at the base of the Kittatinny Mountains, a mile or two from the Appalachian Trail, for forty-eight years, so I know the type of terrain you describe. My area includes farms in the valleys on both sides of the mountain ridge, and deer come down to the open areas to feed. Here, bedding areas are typically found on ridges or on the top of hills just below the ridges. Lakes in mountain hollows are good places to hunt after deer are pressured, but they are poor spots the rest of the year because of the lack of food.

The mature forests have almost no underbrush, which is vital for browse. Dense rhododendron and impenetrable laurel thickets attract pressured deer during the hunting season and over the course of a severe winter. Deer have different bedding and feeding areas, except when acorns are dropping in their bedding areas. In farm fields and open areas, deer have an almost permanent preferred bedding area. In unbroken forested areas, however, deer will shift to be near food sources. Unless some areas have been burned or logged, the population will be low, because there's a lack of food throughout most of the year.

Whitetails prefer white oak acorns in autumn. Put your stand in the white oaks, and you will see deer. Don't worry about occasionally spooking deer—we all do it. They'll be back, particularly when the white oaks are producing bumper crops of acorns. If the white oak acorn crop is poor, which it is three out of every four years, put your stand in the red oaks. Also, do not leave your morning stand until 1 P.M., even if it means delaying lunch. Unpressured deer feed heavily from 11 A.M. to noon, a period most hunters miss because they're heading back to camp for lunch.

In cold weather, deer are usually found on hilltops because the cold settles in the valley.

My Refrigerated Venison Turned Blue in Two Days—Why?

I can't imagine venison spoiling that fast if you were careful in butchering the deer, and you had your refrigerator set at a proper temperature. Something must have gone awry when you processed the meat. I will describe how I process venison, and perhaps you will realize what went wrong.

I field-dress deer as soon as possible because it takes mere minutes for bacteria in a deer's stomach to multiply. With the deer lying on its side, I take my knife and cut a circle around its anus. I then roll the deer on its back and straddle the carcass, keeping its front legs between my legs as I face the rear of the deer. I pull the deer's stomach skin until it reaches its rib cage, and then carefully insert the knife through the skin and make a shallow cut all the way up its pelvic area, being careful not to cut the paunch or intestines. If it's a buck, I then cut around its scrotum and sever the penis.

Next, I take my knife and, cutting to the left of the sternum, I sever all the ribs up to the base of the neck. (Do not cut the skin this high if you are going to have the head mounted.) With the rib cage wide-open, I cut the deer's windpipe and esophagus loose from the rib cage to the backbone. I then lay the deer on its side and pull out the heart, lungs, and diaphragm.

Next, I carefully cut out the kidneys. Being careful not to break the bladder, I then pull the rectum inside through the pelvic area and, in the same motion, roll the deer onto its side so the package of entrails spills out of the deer. I then roll the deer onto its belly and spread its hind legs to let all the blood drain from the body cavity. Finally, I hang the deer up by its neck and spread the ribs open with a stick, which allows the body cavity to cool.

Meat must be cooled before placing it in a refrigerator, and aging meat can only be done properly at a temperature range of 34 to 38 degrees Fahrenheit. If it's colder, the meat will freeze, and if it's warmer, bacteria will multiply and cause spoilage. I skin deer from the neck down. After the hide is off, I use a small propane torch to singe off hair that remains on the carcass. This is the fastest way to clean a carcass.

Great care should be taken to remove the prescapular glands buried in the fat beneath the shoulder blades and the popliteal gland buried in the fat on the forepart of the ham. These glands are gray, about 1-inch long, and, if left intact, can give venison a bad taste and odor. Removing as much fat and tissue as possible will allow you to keep your venison in a freezer more than one year. Fat goes rancid in about six months, even if meat is frozen properly.

Any Advice on Selecting a Camcorder?

I've been shooting professional video for years, but I cannot advise you on the best camcorder for your purpose. There are just too many of them on the market. That said, however, you really can't go wrong with a camera from one of the top makers (Canon, Sony, and so on), especially if you're merely looking to capture wildlife on film.

The difference in price usually just reflects the number of extra features on the camera. It's usually best to research the various brands over the Internet and then make your purchase in person at a camera store. I use a Canon XLIS digital camera, but these run in the $4,000 range. The lens length will be in the vicinity of 10× to 16× and is available with an optical image stabilizer, which is ideal for use without a tripod. Be warned that it is very difficult, if not impossible, to hunt and tape at the same time; you have to do one or the other.

CHAPTER 5

Antlers

What Causes Nontypical Antlers?

Nontypical antlers are not common. I would say fewer than 1 percent of deer have them. Every nontypical is unique, and many nontypical bucks have massive antlers. The drain on a buck's body has to be tremendous and, therefore, huge nontypicals are usually farmland bucks. Bucks living on minimal quality forage are rarely capable of producing such huge racks.

Nontypical antlers are the result of either injury or genetics. If a buck's antlers are injured while in the growing stage, they may develop as nontypical. Ordinarily, the buck will have nontypical antlers for just one or two years and will then go back to growing normal antlers. I know of one buck that grew nontypical racks for three years before he started growing normal antlers again.

I do not know the exact process involved, but antlers do have a "memory." The most extreme example of antler memory I know of is a ten year set of antlers in my collection from a captive buck that badly injured his right antler in a fence when he was a yearling. The antler grew with an almost right-angle curve in it. Every year thereafter, even when he had a large rack, the right antler retained that curve, although it became less pronounced each year.

Growing antlers have a memory, as can be seen by the antlers on this board. The buck broke his antlers as a yearling, and the crooked growth can be seen throughout all ten sets.

I also have proof that some nontypical antlers are the result of genetics. Just as wide-branching or high typical antlers are passed on from father to son, so are some nontypical antlers. Such antlers develop as nontypical without any injuries, proving they are a genetic characteristic. One of the rarest forms of nontypical antlers is the "drop tines." Drop tines can also be found on typical antlers. Drop tines are almost always a genetic characteristic, although I know of one case where one developed through an injury.

Bucks move very little in summer to keep their antlers from being injured while their antlers are soft and growing.

How Long Does It Take for a Buck to Grow Antlers?

It takes about twenty-two weeks for a white-tailed buck to grow a set of antlers. The amount of time he carries his antlers before shedding them is another story. Antler cycles vary by region because different latitudes receive different amounts of sunlight.

Basically, deer south of 33 degrees north latitude grow antlers about two and a half to three months later than deer north of that line. Antler growth among bucks in the same area, however, varies slightly according to each individual's fitness. Bucks coming through the winter in the best condition start growing antlers slightly sooner than bucks that enter spring in poor condition.

Deer in my home area of northwestern New Jersey generally show the first swelling of new antler growth during the first week of April. They show the first shrinking and tightening of velvet, which denotes full antler growth, during the first week in August and shed their velvet during the first week of September.

How Can I Preserve the Velvet?

To answer your question, I consulted my friend Manny Barone, who is a fine taxidermist. First, keep the head cooled below 40 degrees Fahrenheit. You can then have a taxidermist treat the antlers, or do it yourself. Commercial solutions are available from taxidermy supply houses listed in the back of sporting magazines. Manny gets his solutions from Van Dyke Supply Company in Woonsocket, South Dakota. He uses a solution called Preservz-It.

Hang the antlers with the tips hanging down and use a hypodermic needle to inject the solution in a half-dozen spots around the antler bases. The solution will drip to the tips, preserving the velvet. If the head is to be mounted, the cape will have to be salted to preserve it until it can be tanned. Another method immerses the antlers in a solution. The drawback is if the antlers are large; you will need a washtub to put them in, and that takes a lot of solution.

Why Would a Deer Shed Its Antlers in Early December?

I don't think the cold had anything to do with it. Early shedding, while unusual, is not unheard of. In my home area of northwestern New Jersey, bucks in two regions routinely shed their antlers early.

Over most of the country, a buck's antlers are full grown by the middle of August when the velvet starts to dry and shrink.

I was chief gamekeeper for the 6,800-acre Coventry Hunt Club in Warren County for twenty-one years. There was a genetic characteristic in our club's deer herd, and also in a section of Hunterdon County where I did a lot of deer photography. Some of the biggest bucks in these areas dropped their antlers the last week of November or the first week of December. We knew they were bucks because we could see the raw pedicles, but we couldn't shoot them because they didn't have the required 3 inches of antler. One time I shot a buck that lost both of his antlers when he hit the ground after the shot. Thankfully, I had the antlers for proof in case I was checked by a warden.

Bucks' antlers evolved to mesh with those of rivals, helping to prevent damage to the combatants.

Another time I shot a buck and had an antler pop off when I grabbed it to drag him from the woods. The earliest record I have of a big buck shedding his antlers was in Hunterdon County, New Jesey, on November. 25. I believe genetics plays a major role in when and where a buck will shed his antlers.

Do "Sticker Points" Serve a Purpose?

Sticker points are a genetic characteristic. Most deer don't have them, but where they appear, many bucks seem to have them, presumably because the trait is passed on by the area's dominant buck. Sticker points also seem to be a characteristic of age, because bucks seldom develop sticker points until they are at least two and a half years old. Once a buck develops sticker points, he usually produces them from then on.

Although sticker points aren't needed, bucks use them while making rubs. Most of the bark removed from a sapling during rubbing is done with the antler burr or with the knurling at the bases. The older the buck, the higher and rougher the ridge of knurling becomes. Sticker points provide even more surface area to rub with, letting a buck gouge much deeper into the wood. Some sticker points, however, prevent the buck from bringing its antler burr in contact with the sapling.

What's the Longest Tine You've Measured?

I once measured a spike that had curving beam that measured about 18 inches. The longest tine I've measured growing from a main beam is $11^3/4$ inches. I have heard of tines as long as 14 inches, but I have not personally measured any that long. Unfortunately, the Boone and Crockett record book does not include tine length with its entries.

What Causes an Increase in Spike Buck Numbers?

Most spikes are the result of malnutrition. I believe if a spike buck can get a protein diet of 16 percent to 18 percent, he will have the ability to subsequently grow a nice rack. That can be accomplished by reducing the entire herd, greatly reducing the doe population, or planting nutritious food patches. Research proves that genes from

The bucks make a visual sign when they expose the white inner wood while making a rub on a sapling.

genetically inferior deer can be passed on and the offspring will be inferior, even when given a high-protein diet. Ordinarily, inbreeding doesn't happen in wild deer, but if the big bucks have been shot and a few genetically inferior bucks are doing the breeding, it can account for the increase in spikes.

Why Are Pennsylvania Deer Getting Smaller on Average?

Pennsylvania deer are getting smaller because the herd has gotten so large. The latest estimate I heard put the deer population in Pennsylvania at 1.5 million. The deer are literally eating themselves out of house and home. They are consuming the forests and preventing any regrowth. There is very little inbreeding in wild deer because young bucks usually disperse beyond their mothers' home

No one can explain why bucks have drop tines like those on this buck's antlers.

ranges when they are one to one and a half years old. Most disperse at least 5 miles. A dominant buck might breed his daughters and granddaughters because they all stay within their home range, but even that's unlikely because few bucks live to be four or five years old.

Because of the huge deer population and related problems, Gary Alt, Pennsylvania's former deer project leader, has proposed a new concept for the state. Instead of holding the antlerless deer season after the breeding season, he proposes moving it to October before the breeding season. His reasoning is correct, and if it comes to pass, it will be closely monitored by other states with similar deer problems. He reasoned that if you are going to shoot does, why not shoot them before the bucks run themselves ragged through tending and fighting. Bucks that survive gun season will then go into winter in better shape. With fewer does to breed, more does will be bred in the first rut between November 10 and

November 17 and thus have their fawns earlier in the spring. It is a well-known fact that early fawns will be larger in body size as adults and have a better chance of surviving their first winter.

What Are the Best Trophy States?

Many regions produce big bucks, but most are top agricultural states, such as Iowa. Iowa leads the United States in Boone and Crockett Club entries, with eight bucks among B&C's top fifty whitetails of all time. Saskatchewan also has eight top-fifty bucks, including the Milo Hanson buck, which is the number-one B&C typical. Minnesota, which used to be the number-one state, has seven top-fifty entries. Western Wisconsin's bluff country is also a top-notch area for B&C whitetails.

Overall, northern states produce the biggest bucks because they have the largest subspecies *Odocoileus virginianus dakotensis* and *borealis*. The largest northern deer usually come from rich farmland, because the superior food allows for better body and antler growth. Wilderness deer often grow older than farm-country deer, but vast forests seldom have the rich diet vital for maximum body and antler growth. Although many record-class bucks come from the same areas, don't ignore areas with fewer B&C entries. Record bucks are not flukes. A big buck's presence indicates the area holds quality food and genetics.

What Plantings Promote Antler Growth?

The cheapest and most effective thing you can do is lime your fields heavily. The plants will pick up calcium and, in turn, the deer that eat the crops will have higher calcium levels. Alfalfa, clover, and birdsfoot trefoil are favored deer foods. Hire your county farm agent to test your soil, and then fertilize food plot crops following his recommendations. The deer will benefit from the phosphorus, nitrogen, and potash in the fertilizer. Improving the soil improves antler and body size.

Why Are Deer on My Property Breaking Their Racks?

Your property, as you describe it under your program of quality deer management, might seem like a whitetail paradise, but its soil might lack calcium. Have your county soil agent test your soil and

*Most fights only last a few seconds because it doesn't take much longer
than that to prove the dominant buck's superiority.*

make recommendations for liming and fertilizing. Your management program, however, is more likely the culprit. Before you
started QDM, perhaps only one big buck roamed your area. That
buck's dominance quite likely prevented fighting, because smaller
bucks would not have challenged the hierarchy. Now that your
property supports many big bucks, fights are more common.
What's more, because the bucks are larger and stronger, they're
more likely to break antlers.

I Found a Heavily Chewed Antler in December— Should I Be "Shed Hunting" Earlier?

The heavily chewed antler was probably dropped a year before you
discovered it. I don't believe rodents could consume that much of
the antler if it was dropped that winter. Although mice usually
begin chewing antlers soon after they fall, they consume only the
tips of the tines in the first month.

If your area doesn't have snow cover, start shed-hunting in early February. Many northerners wait a little longer, but only because snow is still covering the ground. Warm weather often makes deer carry their antlers longer.

Typically, as the weather cools in November, a deer's metabolism begins slowing. In the North, this slowdown bottoms out in early December, when deer have reduced their food intake 50 percent to 60 percent. Contrary to popular belief, cold—not day length—causes this change. This relates to antler shedding because warm weather delays the metabolic slowdown, letting deer maintain a higher metabolism longer and consume more food. Better-nourished bucks usually carry their antlers longer. As a rule of thumb, begin looking for shed antlers as soon as the ground is bare enough to see them. Any disturbance you make won't push deer out of the area.

This Spring I Saw a Deer Whose Pedicles Were Almost Covered by Skin—Is This Unusual?

Bucks in our area of northern New Jersey drop their antlers between late December and late January, with some carrying their antlers into February. The white antler base will dry, scab over, and turn brown within twenty-four hours. The surrounding skin starts to grow over the pedicle immediately, but takes a month to six weeks to completely cover the pedicle. That new skin is the start of the velvet. The first sign of growth—swelling on top of the pedicle—is usually visible the first week in April. Growth starts slowly, but speeds up in May, when as much as $1/8$ to $1/4$ inch of new growth is added daily.

Also, as for the white spot you described seeing on the buck's ham, it could be genetic, but I think it was probably caused by a puncture wound. I have seen many examples on different types of animals, including humans, where an injury to the skin killed nerve endings in the dermis, causing hair to grow white on that part from then on.

My 10-Point Buck Had Dry Velvet in Mid-November—Why?

Ordinarily, bucks shed their velvet in September. I have seen, however, about twelve bucks retain their velvet throughout the season.

These bucks did not attempt to rub the velvet off or simply couldn't do so.

Usually, when a buck keeps dried velvet on his antlers, it is because of an injury or illness. From your description, however, I doubt that was the case. I know of two bucks, one a whitetail and one a mule deer, that had this condition. In the case of the mule deer, I saw the buck in 1995 and 1997, and I assume he retained his velvet in 1996. Judging from this and the fact both bucks appeared healthy, I believe it was a genetic characteristic, which would explain why it happened repeatedly. I have also theorized the bucks sustained earlier injuries and recovered, but their antlers retained a "memory" of the injury in preceding years. I, however, have no proof of this.

What Criteria Differentiate Typical and Nontypical Racks?

To be accepted into the Boone and Crockett record books, a whitetail must score 170 typical or 195 nontypical. To be accepted into the Pope and Young record books, a whitetail must score 125 typical or 150 nontypical. Hunters can choose which category their deer is judged in. If a rack has more than 25 inches of nontypical points on a typical frame, it's best judged as a nontypical. That's because the nontypical points would be deducted from the typical score.

Should We Hunt Spikes and Does to Increase Quality Buck Numbers?

Overcrowding and sufficient but not nutritious food usually result in spikes or small forks in white-tailed bucks. Genetics also play a lesser role in antler development; and some spike bucks have deficient genes, as was proven in research at the Kerrville Texas Research Station.

It started a nationwide killing of spike bucks in the name of good deer management. Many overlooked the fact, however, that Texas, before that time, had a law prohibiting the harvest of spike bucks. If a buck had deficient genes, and some did, they lived and become old enough to breed. This situation was not occurring in other states because spike bucks were legal game, and therefore were killed before becoming breeders.

Because of the branching on each of this buck's G-2 tines, he would lose points if judged by Boone and Crockett rules in the Typical category.

When the Texas law was changed, the problem was partially solved. This, however, masked the real problem. The problems persisted in other states where spike bucks were not protected. I visited the research station in Kerrville shortly after the findings were published. The researchers acknowledged they had proven some spike bucks were genetically deficient, but they noted that a lack of nutrition more often caused spike antlers. Shooting spikes was merely the quick fix. The problem was, is, and always will be the availability of sufficient, nutritious food.

In other cases across the South, spikes are usually late-born fawns, and have no genetic deficiencies. Give them another year, and they'll start producing better racks. The deer population in North America, excluding Mexico, is around 30 million. There are more deer now than in pre-Columbian times, and we have an excess in some areas. To extensively study the food that a deer eats, compare it with preferred foods from fifty years ago. You will find the lists to be extremely different. What a deer eats as preferred food today might only be what is predominately available.

When the herd is below the land's carrying capacity, deer can pick and choose between various foods, eating only the most nutritious. When the deer population explodes and the number of deer exceeds what the area can produce, the most desirable and nutritious plants are eliminated. According to Pennsylvania state foresters, the overpopulation of its deer herd has changed the entire makeup of the forest. Different plants, shrubs, and trees now grow in areas that used to support other vegetation.

What is the answer? Shoot more does. If you have to reduce the herd further, shoot spikes. To produce quality deer, you need abundant nutritious food, which won't exist until the population is in check. But even supplemental feeding won't solve the problem. Social stress from overcrowding also hurts antler growth. One reason trophy deer management fails is that most hunters and the public want lots of deer. But as long as you have a lot of deer eating a lot of food, there won't be many trophy bucks. A one-and-a-half-year-old buck weighing 140 pounds is respectable for that age bracket. But if that buck was also a 6 pointer, it would be well on its way to being a trophy buck.

Living on good farmland, this six-month-old fawn is big for his age. His first set of antlers will probably be 6 points.

Do Antlers Indicate a Deer's Age?

Antler growth involves a number of variables such as genetics and nutrition, so antler size provides only a rough estimate of age. Antlers do not grow uniformly, nor are they guaranteed to get larger every year. The only part of the antler that grows consistently is the base, which fits into the pedicle socket. This base increases in circumference each year even when antler mass does not. I tried to devise a formula for aging deer by measuring the bases of hundreds of known-age antlers, but there was too much variation.

As a rough basis, I found the antler base on a one-and-a-half-year-old buck to be between 22 and 26 millimeters. The difference is attributable to variations in genetics and food sources. The base increases by 2 to 4 millimeters per year. You must have the antler in your hand to get this measurement, but it is the only constant in antler growth.

Some folks try to age deer by measuring the antler an inch above the burr. This, however, isn't consistent either. I have a set of 11 antlers mounted from a known-age buck. At $1^1/_2$ years, the antlers measured 20 millimeters; at $2^1/_2$, 24; $3^1/_2$, 30; $4^1/_2$, 33; $5^1/_2$, 38; $6^1/_2$, 38; $7^1/_2$, 41; $8^1/_2$, 38; $9^1/_2$, 38; $10^1/_2$, 39; and $11^1/_2$, 38. Unfortunately, I did not measure the antler bases before having these antlers mounted.

In May I Saw a Buck with Velvet Antlers That Were at Least Two Inches Thick—Will They Be That Big This Fall?

If the buck you saw had velvet antlers that were more than 2 inches in diameter in May, you should hope to see him during hunting season. He will have a large rack when his antlers are grown. You should keep in mind the diameter of velvet antlers can be deceiving. The velvet hairs on a growing set of antlers can be as long as $^1/_8$ inch. Further, the velvet skin, when filled with blood, is also about $^1/_{16}$-inch thick. Therefore, antlers that appear to be 2 inches in diameter are probably more like $1^1/_2$ inches. The rack will still be impressive, but not as massive as you thought.

Many hunters mistakenly use the terms "antlers" and "horns" interchangeably; there is, however, a difference. Cows grow horns. Deer grow antlers. Horns are made of keratin and grow continuously throughout an animal's life. All of the growth is nourished from blood vessels in the core of the horn. Thus, a horn grows from the inside out. Antlers are pure bone. Initially, the antler is nourished from blood vessels going up through the center of the antler; and they are also supplied with blood vessels that run on the outside of the antler through the velvet. As the antlers get larger, the internal blood flow shuts down. From there, antlers are nourished from the outside in. Antlers grow like a tree—with new growth added to the tips—instead of like grass where the growth is in the bottom, pushing the entire structure upward.

To see a group of bucks like this would gladden the heart of every hunter.

Why Do Some Bucks Have More Antler Growth Than Others in the Summer?

Antler growth is stimulated by photoperiodism, the lengthening of the daylight hours in a twenty-four-hour period. Therefore, you would think that all deer living in the same area and eating the same food, would start growing their antlers at the same time. Unfortunately, it doesn't happen that way.

Mature bucks are the first to grow antlers, shed velvet, and cast antlers. When all other factors, such as food and age, are equal, the difference is genetics. I once observed a buck that carried his antlers two months longer than another buck; and he started growing his antlers about six weeks after the other buck. Both bucks, however, shed their velvet at the same time.

An important point to remember is two bucks that cast their antlers at the same time don't necessarily start growing new ones at the same time. The diameter of growing antlers increases only slightly as they continue to lengthen. Most of the mass is formed early, and future growth goes toward the length of the main beam and tines.

My Buck Had Palmated Brow Tines, and the Antlers Turned Out to be Hollow—Is This Common?

Although it is rare, bucks can grow palmated—or webbed—brow tines. I have never heard, or even read, however, of hollow antlers. Therefore, the rack you have is most unusual. Antlers grow from the outside in with bone salts being deposited by the blood vessels that are in the velvet. The bone salts—calcium, magnesium, and phosphorus—are taken from a buck's skeleton. After the antlers have grown, the softer center of the antler, known as the sporangium, is filled.

When the antlers are fully grown, they begin to harden and solidify from the base to the tips and from the outside, inside. On the other hand, horns—such as those on bulls and rams—grow from the inside out. Once removed from an animal, horns can take on a hollow appearance if the inside core is left to dry and then removed.

I Saw a Buck with Hard, Polished Antlers in July— Do Bucks Always Shed?

What you saw was most unusual. Under normal conditions, a buck's antlers are full grown in velvet by the end of July; and they begin to harden by the first week of August. Most bucks rub the dried velvet from their antlers by the first week of September.

I know of two situations when bucks don't shed their antlers. The first scenario involves a buck's pineal gland. This gland, located in the brain, is often referred to as a deer's "third eye." It is the receptor for electrical impulses generated by optic nerves. If injured, the pineal gland can be prevented from signaling the pituitary gland to increase or decrease the amount of testosterone produced and distributed throughout a buck's body. It is the increased amount of testosterone in August that causes antlers to solidify. A decrease in testosterone leads to antler shedding. A buck could also keep his antlers if he was somehow castrated, by accident or gunshot, and the injury occurred after the antlers had hardened.

How do Mineral Blocks Affect Antler Growth?

Trace minerals are important to all animals throughout the year. Deer cannot maximize or reach their full body size, weight, and antler development without proper minerals. I provide deer with mineral supplements year-round, but they visit the sites the least during the rut, which in New Jersey runs from mid-October to mid-December. During that time, bucks are more concerned with breeding than eating. Whitetails consume supplemental minerals heavily from mid-March through summer, when bucks are growing new antlers and does are producing and nursing fawns.